MW00907902

AN ABSENCE
SO GREAT
AND
SPONTANEOUS
IT IS
EVIDENCE
OF
LIGHT

ANNE GORRICK

the operating system print//document

AN ABSENCE SO GREAT AND SPONTANEOUS IT IS EVIDENCE OF LIGHT

ISBN: 978-1-946031-30-3
Library of Congress Control Number: 2018948543
copyright © 2018 by Anne Gorrick
edited and designed by Lynne DeSilva-Johnson

is released under a Creative Commons CC-BY-NC-ND (Attribution, Non Commercial, No Derivatives) License: its reproduction is encouraged for those who otherwise could not afford its purchase in the case of academic, personal, and other creative usage from which no profit will accrue.

Complete rules and restrictions are available at:
http://creativecommons.org/licenses/by-nc-nd/3.0/

For additional questions regarding reproduction, quotation, or to request a pdf for review contact
operator@theoperatingsystem.org

This text was set in LGf Besitos Round, Wet Arial, Sharpy, Europa, Gill Sans, Minion, Franchise, and OCR-A Standard.
Cover Art by Lynne DeSilva-Johnson
Cover uses a photograph of the author shot by Peter Genovese

Books from The Operating System are distributed to the trade by SPD/Small Press Distribution, with ePub and POD via Ingram, with production by Spencer Printing, in Honesdale, PA, in the USA.

2018-19 OS System Operators
CREATIVE DIRECTOR/FOUNDER/MANAGING EDITOR: Lynne DeSilva-Johnson
DEPUTY EDITOR: Peter Milne Greiner
CONTRIBUTING EDITORS: Kenning JP Garcia, Adrian Silbernagel
JOURNEYHUMAN / SYSTEMS APPRENTICE: Anna Winham
SOCIAL SYSTEMS / HEALING TECH: Curtis Emery
VOLUNTEERS and/or ADVISORS: Adra Raine, Alexis Quinlan, Clarinda McLow, Bill Considine, Careen Shannon, Joanna C. Valente, Michael Flatt, L. Ann Wheeler, Jacq Greyja

The Operating System is a member of the Radical Open Access Collective, a community of scholar-led, not-for-profit presses, journals and other open access projects. Now consisting of 40 members, we promote a progressive vision for open publishing in the humanities and social sciences. Learn more at: http://radicaloa.disruptivemedia.org.uk/about/

Your donation makes our publications, platform and programs possible! We <3 You.
bit.ly/growtheoperatingsystem

the operating system
141 Spencer Street #203
Brooklyn, NY 11205
www.theoperatingsystem.org
operator@theoperatingsystem.org

AN ABSENCE
SO GREAT
AND
SPONTANEOUS
IT IS
EVIDENCE
OF
LIGHT

ACKNOWLEDGEMENTS AND GRATITUDE

10,000 thanks to those that helped this work into being: Lori Anderson Moseman, Lynn Behrendt, Steve Cotten, Kathleen Gilligan, Maria Gorrick, Robert Kelly, Maryrose Larkin, Charlotte Mandell, John Bloomberg-Rissman, Michael Ruby and Eileen Tabios and all the friends and editors who published this work early on. 10,000 more thanks to my husband Peter Genovese. Lastly, this book's body comes into being as a result of Lynne DeSilva-Johnson's art, sweat and vision at the OS. Thank you, Lynne.

Some of these poems have appeared in the following journals:

Altered Scale, Anthem, the Bangalore Review, Big Bridge, Birds Piled Loosely, Cricket, EOAGH, the Helios Mss, La Vague, Otoliths, the Otter, Poetry Wales, Poets on the Great Recession, Journal of Radical Light, Reality Beach, Shearsman Magazine, Sprung Poems, Tears in the Fence, Truck (guest-edited by Michael Rothenberg), *Upstairs at Duroc, Wag's Revue, Waymark: Voices of the Valley, where is the river: a poetry experiment* and *word for/word.*

The poems "A Table Full of Interest" and "Rub Synonyms for Bad" were translated into Spanish by Eduardo Padilla and appeared respectively in *Transtierros* and *La Presa.*

CONTENTS

out of sleep the poem
opens its dazzling whispering hands

'THE POEM' *by* GEORGE OPPEN
from *PRIMITIVE*

Nimblewilled Android Pineboy
She suffers from brisket syndrome, mechanical suggestion
Kiss the snot otter in a hard hat
and then tell a story about your stuff
Antic dinky animation in a blue sea
The numerous definitions of pipes
Smirky and then there were fewer
Rash on hands or brittle bone disease on Nylon TV
Herpes travels to a science center as Brineshrimpdirect
The shape of milk knits a scene
Indeed India and Smokesmash Robinson
The skinny girl margarita IS the color of New Jersey
or a shantybisque all inked up
Understones, understories
Stylistic devices describe a stiltsville for sale
Storkcraft or Storm King?
An Italian translation in insensibility, water loss, riskmetrics
She snorts Xanax, bath salts, Adderall, Vicodin
Minks by the hedge, her pink blinker fluid
Atlantis, Atlantic City, Hersey Park, Bermuda, Bergdorf Goodman
And then Minty the Candy Cane fell down on the ground dancing to his Mintymix
Tiny chats under tiny umbrellas, skyrim and grey
Mistakes were made, there was brainwashing in Avalon on Singapore Airlines
Voltaire, iridium, slingbox, slime soccer, slipknot slinky
The wild, the gloss, the woods
Daylight savings, dictionary, dark spores
Spark notes, speed test, dried firewood for sale
Libélula dresses, skirt steaks, the history of pi
Iconic memory like her limbs falling asleep
Byzantine photobiographies of Nellie Bly
Temperature conversions and tremulous definitions rattle a Texas town
Here we have a machine entombed by a lyric
or a lyric entombed by a machine

This poem was written after my poem "Kinky Vinyl" as it was suggested by Google.

STARFISH SLANG

Robot unicorn attack Regretsy
not remotely steampunk
Whimsicle fuckery, dead things, Grooveshark sanctum
Medea's big happy family
Arsenal invincibles, injuries
Arrears Avoidance program
Enraged regeneration
Regalèssia writhings
with arsenic on the Etruscans footprints
Arson anthem
Solar anus, solar animal solar and heliospheric observatory
illesteva-pipe-kimchi-kool-man-repeller
The Water Club, the way she wobbles on aggressive skates
agrees with the tomatometer, agrees with the moon
The way a mineral splits, grenade chords, learnscape
A slanderer's bible for angry birds
Androgen insensitivity syndrome
Reason #5:
addicting games, adrenal fatigue
Gonads and strife, starfish slang, secreted squirrels, sneezing pandas
Ghosts pout, and death is no parenthesis, Peshat and Derash
Her hair was in a ponytail, dangle sauce
Radar algorithms, algae rockfish, algae geek
Galaxy tab, gallbladder, Galileo, Galapagos
Anagram your anatomy
in deer antler velvet

This poem was written after my poem "A Gardener's Rearranged Sun" as it was suggested by Google.

Needles and necklaces
Wing nomenclature
Sea wing nova, pearl mist theory
Threadless thrillist
From throw pillows to throat cancer
Throne of the four winds
Throughput through a dog's ear
A thousand dreams, a trauma lens, a tantrum's thin haze
How to get through a timeshare presentation?
Red mango, the Drawing Center, the Drunk Diet
Foreshadowings, carmines, carpaccio
Carpet of the sun, of snow, outgassing, clover fractions
Fracture and failure ulcerates, of frantic breastfeeding, frantic redhead
The dream hotel
The dream of the burning boy at Wicker Park
Whip my hair, what are those white things in my throat?
A white thick toenail, or a white throated sparrow?
White then pink
White then brown
And then nothing turned itself inside out
Not without salt, not what my hands have done
Carbide wedding bands and their unusual facts
Tungsten-lined underwear
Undrugged and undressed
Bright skies, black wings, belly button tickling again
High-fructose corn syrup, Hiroshima, high-speed rail
Judgement against history, histrionic histamines
Hands and tongue song
Handwriting without tears
Stardoll, starfall, Stellarium
Hunger games, Scranton, scaffolding
Scatter plot, scatter analysis
Diffraction, barcharts

Even the flowers pick themselves
A continuous lean, a couple of poor Polish-speaking Romanians
A color that starts with the letter S, D, H, J, F, or K
A colored ion generally indicates an array
Field flow fractionation, flung onto snow
Plenty of fish, please touch, pleaser shoes
Negative calorie foods, negligent embalming, primrose dresses
An Italian straw hat, fracture atlas, fairy tales
Neopets, terrorbirds, the summary of a woman

This poem was written after my poem "Titania/Titanium: a Wedding" as it was suggested by Google.

When not to use a hand sanitizer, or go to China, or order fish
When notating pitch, when notated music was invented
Notational velocity, notated clothing
Cheap flights for Chinese New Year
The execute permission was denied the object
He expects her to chase him, that Gregor Mendel
in the Year of the Rabbit, reddish brown
Reddish urine, reddish brown hair, reddish egret
with textual evidence:
lamp, paper, theory
Technique Tuesday
Florence and the Machine flourished in copperplate
Or a few dollars more, or a woman like you, or a gringo like me
or a reasonable facsimile thereof, or a beautiful nightmare
Hero or tyrant, law or theory, look or touch, a grass or a tree, a skill or a talent
Evening dresses, everyday food, Eventbrite
Sevendust, small animals walk through their definitions, bodies found in a trunk in Arizona
Bodies found in a hollow tree reveal their motion in water
Cry for water, a silvered oiled glory
Traces of your friends fracture around the favored mind
When your computer sleeps and notifications appear
When will a crocodile eat the sun?
When a couple breaks up, when cows lie down
when even a single syllable cannot be pronounced
A comparison of two numbers by division
When prose accommodates action
his composition would almost always end with a hero, smoking

An atmosphere of bones and notebooks, her Venus bones
A synonym perceives itself as warm and caring
It's always sunny and deductible in Philadelphia
where a wedding is like a jungle filled with candy

Aerobic respiration over the sea, chaos is a way to acknowledge her partiture
An orca pulls a Sea World trainer to her death
Harm harmonizes with her hair
Trail patterns, manipulations
Her mouth without tears like a party favor
Paralyzed man implant, the shape of hands
She bathes in snakes and snapdragons
What is the prince's name in Snow White?
Leopard Ice Cream predicts that some reality shows are entirely fake
Expressibles, extreme couponing
Use "homemade firearms" in a sentence
Benign positional vertigo, an album of competitive advantage
One of Satan's autobiographies is called "Ice"
Collective bargaining for nouns
Prayer collects blood from the head and arms
Collect tropics, transient failure, the disease that slips inside pictures
Cherubs are born and then they are rented or bought
A thousand clowns and the way each one will die
What is that thing next to your blood vessel?
Things that end with the letter D
Engadgeted and enchanted, her heart enlarged by his blonde
Enlivened by the mystery of rock powders
She is a borderless instrument
Fat calculators, magic calculators
Salt glow hives, hidden object games, sallow and inappropriate
Pandora's bracelets, cloud virgins, sea rays
The Swedish coastline sways in the summer breeze, septic
Drowned wolf swag, their auras wickedly melded together
Atonement rises like a mystery vacation
River salon, there were slots in her decisions
A traversal creates pairs of slipping fish
Chariots pale as character actors, the orientalism of living things
Types of turquoise and the misuse of spiritual gifts
Behaviors of the gifted and their properties of gold
A skilled use of hydrogen, the misery of bubbles and time
An experiment with magnets and eggs at a science fair
What to do at home with light?

Christ recycles minerals, Siamese fighting fish work on memory
Patterns of arrangement, grain the size of lyric
An emergent severity index
Dragonoid chance, de-Cocteau this poem
Complete the table for this metabolic equation
Wooden hearted poems canceled in full episodes
Notational velocity, paper defines
The stars test drive our hearts, wind daylilies into the body
Beach holidays border on nutrition
She speaks like her body temperature is below normal
Massage her like burnt oak, build a fire of verbs
Absent from her own soliloquies, she pleases precisely
Play with almonds, a bee playing cards
Threadless milk cake, an apartment in a meadow
Dispersion, availability, flour spreads, firewood forecasts accuracy
Flammability, five dreamings, five fingered death punch
Five women wore the same dress, willow wished
Spiked heels and eggrolls, seedpages
Cut an orange into five quarters
What is normal saline? A patient climbs the stairs: starfall stratosphere
Antecedent consequence, crows fly, a cold front passes, unprocessed items
Firearms as a collection of nouns

This poem was written after my poem "An Envelope Full of Music/A Contingent Event"
as it was suggested by Google.

THIS MOVIE IS BROKEN

Of course lions dance, my bright little star
You're still single
You can pay me back in gum
You can call it love or thunder
Her pearls drink milk in the dark
Can Calphalon go in the oven?
Can Call of Duty zombies be beat?
Fake calla lilies and fake chickens
Sleep lyrically wraps spring
Her lupus, her Lucky Strikes, her lumineers
She is branded by luck
Luminarc, landscapes marketed by radiant mystery
Luminous fish effect, whiskey park, wheelworks
A tiara of molecular substance
Which is bigger? Better? An example of
Is Kevjumba a heterosexual bear wrestler?
Is Banksy Jewish, gay, white, black, pregnant or contagious?
Is beer vegan?
Is beautiful a curse or a noun?
The hard part of Burgundy is beach bum tanning on Stranger TV
Burnout lasers: a synonym for skin, a southcloud
The Beautiful Soup Theater Collective
The odd rubies in female interest, infectious diseases, frostwire
Otterbox and desert cities
What's another word for Sunday?
Idioms, Iditarod, the ideal weight of her identity
I need some prank, I need cute hair, I am Number 4
From Prada to Nada
I pulled a muscle loving you
Basement wilderness, the warpwoods, horoscope
The ethnic aesthetics of consumption
I really love my bank commercial, I really like you in Korean
Long words, light periods, lame jokes
Birth control running shoes quotes – this is why we're fat

Her bones begin this sentence
Tattoos, abortions, ma pêche – How expensive is Plan B?
Her vocabulary is made of metal and foam – her vocal range was like a farm
Heated driveways exhale in Tokyo
Which elements can expand their octet?
Can you freeze milk? Can you get mono twice?

You find yourself in a room, but you forgot the blueberries
You find a ticket on the dash and you collide
You find yourself in the middle of a frozen lake

She eats a wayback burger
Spasms splash succulent surgery fusion suction
Maplestory
Greek letters sewn together wrong
Her eyelashes were sewn on
Books nurse scorned timber, beloved as the sky
Scorned Woman Hot Sauce
The gold he sought in translation
Throwing knives and throwing up blood:
there's a wolf assassin in Togetherville
Parts of speech pitchfork sets of attraction
Perfect harmony performed by intruders
Personal Christmas ornaments, personality disordered
Personal oxygen bar and oracle
Inordinate ladies origami-ed together
The anatomy of angels must be comprised of plant cells
What is an "I" word to describe you?
Hourglasses and alcoholics and errata
Organisms that reproduce asexually have the ability
for their exoskeletons to benefit agriculture
Is this poem an event that decreases the behavior that precedes it?
Event mining, the mimic octopus
This sentence is camouflaged in adaptation
presocial and post-colonial, mockery and hybridity
Darkness symboled in lyric, her sadness splitscreen
Splice comma splice, sunlight in miniature
Splintered adjective, splintered light, splintered angel

The history of wood is bone
a soundtrack to sincerity, broken white lines

Cohesion and coherent light
Poems are temporal oscillations
His breath: a monochromatic light, a temper trap
The sun over a New York's deciduous forest
The sounds in Shrubland: this sentence and its soundclouds
Lyrics soaked with screaming, snoring, throwing up
Insects, questions, birds, things
Some of us never die
Some odd rubies came running
Some quadrilaterals are rectangles
Drug antagonists, property anxiety, some weirdness termed "fundamental"
The physics of solace, theories entangled in their jumping
I am your radio slave, your repairer, your radiation pressure noise
I am your radiant history of the sea
Irradiance, their ashes as seen on TV
Summary, Sparknotes, text, gavotte
Walk to class at a constant speed

Do your scars wait for god? Or makeup for monsters?
Or you for my theory of the dead man?
If you were meant for me, then you won't feel a thing
You wanted to be a memory
I cast shadows in your interrupted lyrics
Saturdays flirt in Italian
Shoes and skin sleep in a Tokyo hotel
on apricot scatter, obituary obscura
Scattered order adjusts terminology
Muscle, fracture, asymptote, angles, exercises, strategies
These lines strain at definition
Thrust fault, thoracic spine, mountain goats, love chords
Throwing and thinking inside a cathedral
The yellow pages tell her that this is the year of the rabbit
Evershade, explosions in the sky
When the phone is an experiment in international living
Is aspirin a verb? Astronomy?

Performance art as an intervention in probability
Her beetroot utopia, a sheltered logic for pigs
Silvercyst, oatmeal, gold in suspension, osmotic pressure
Underworld, undertone, underoath, undercovers
Under the pressure of darkness
Suspicion, dishwater, silk, spinning lights
His shoulder blades under spiritual construction
Alcohol and ghosts: Spirits-A-Go-Go
Animal spirits are a bestiary of the commons
A bivalent chromatin structure marked
Does she make pearls in her shells?
Her oyster ligaments draw and dredge
Look up in your dream dictionary shutters and sunlight
An intolerable blue gloss on his marvelous arms
Morning glory, the morning after pill, sickness and ratings
Endless engagement rings in their enchanted leaning
The entropy of dogs, their uncertainty principal, their fortunetelling gravity
Our dependency on code and the color blue
on the unreachable, unreadable calendar
Wait for the Royal Caribbean unicorn attack
Oranges, orchids, roses, origami, order, origin
Our sorting technologies appall
They're swaggerific, capable of swallowing a knife
Swallow your gum, or swallow the sun or stones
a fishbone, a tooth, a pint of blood, a battery
until your ears pop
(dagger vomit, ear heart)
Cherry blossom the hollow
Get on the Peter Pan bus
Bring your frost emblems and your prehistoric terror

This poem was written after a worksheet of Lynn Behrendt's first book titles as it was suggested by Google.

SHE IS FRAYED AND TURNING BLUE

She invented revenge
breast calcifications, broken overcast in a theater of rain
She also invented love, absolute sound, the abacus group, absence, an abandoned reef
Sew crafty, so busted, so serious
as if she was a symbol or sacrament in Francis Bacon
She is staggeringly high
She's not a Christian and she doesn't have an MBA
The absurdity of solace in this salt
She is not marked as serializable
A soft moon paws at its surroundings
She is not a symbolic link to a mismanaged object

The pink truths inside a pistol case, pill identification
Insert princess here

She serves doubt into your heart while she writes on her arms
a blue uncertain stumbling buzz
She's a black ops blue valentine, a quilled ocean strategy
She scatters definitions around like birds or black and whites
Sleep shapes itself to her, like pillows shaped like animals
Is sushi healthy? Is strep throat contagious?
Her vertebral column, the intersection of a Super Moon with a silken diagonal Barcelona
People are sometimes shattered by their clothing
the sheet music in their shoulders
Arousal theory, symbol, sentence, synonym
She can be fatal, sex-linked, accurate, her white waters turning into marbles
Her carnations become transparent
while skiing or sleeping
while I hope in Italian
while I high-five sinners and hop in the DeLorean
I heard you paint houses
Milky Way migraine, mouth open
My tongue hurts to swallow, my head is numb
My Little Pony is in ruins
Sugargloss, lipstick jungle, sugarmouth, angelpalace

My agnostic swag, Limewire
Her hands spin around like myth, palm trees fall asleep easily
always cold, are burning in allegiant air
A ringed eruption of the fingers, each happiness ringed by lions
Easter, kanji like a dream, like a universe in review
A convention of signs, slab barriers, silence
Slogan deflection, petaling, foamflowers, red thorns
Cherry echo, Earl Grey tea
Ghost jackals lament in congruent prayer
Exorcisms and certain supplications remembering that meat loves salt
Punctuate epitheial keratopathy
Sonata, starry, moonletters, sky bleach
Night wish and sweat
Her stars, her pleasure, her insistence, her sable dome, her theater
Trick sizes, she dances like Mussolini, like an organization
No hands, dynamite, jar of hearts, rhapsodize, rhyme
She is a rhythm dictionary
Rhetoric, stone sour, slow turning chords like electric motors
Outpatient, magnesiums, pale folklore: grey
Skin and its causes
Screaming without makeup on Interval Radio
Embered skies haze, photons in Eden
A necklace of neutrons, nonlinear optics
Smell this jade, minerals imagine a feast
Bare legs, bare lymphocytes
Trees should not look like this
Sheet music sheds leaves, shades bark
Brain Pop, stencil, shower curtain, Scappoose
Secret Lenten seasons, seamless hemispheres
Her space holiday, her morning elegance, her fearful symmetry
fingerspelled in lettuce, rice and salt

This poem was written after an anonymous poem I found online
"She is not a servant to scattered branches" as it was suggested by Google

AN AMNESIA PRAYER

A rarely executed move in chess, a rarely seen animal
this side of a Rauschenberg shift
Assemble language
Florescent flutter, flash idiom, fractional pollen
Flippant, flirt, eyelash slang, A-flat minor, a flood of paper, campfires
Camera-ism without a name, without limits or rage or pain
or training wheels or supervision
Witch hazel profiles temptations, provocations
Papillon, Narcolepsy Magazine, readymade breakup, an old cadence
An event of geographical ethics in spaces of affect
Event opal, postcolonial shame, grammatology
at international intervals, nouns never sleep and are not compounded
Pre-owned wedding dresses, preoccipital notch, styles of preoccupied attachment
Thoughts of the self and food in 1985
Approval matrix, are art and joke synonyms?
Scary maze game, Vinyl King, search the sheets for static
Strobist, words containing the letters Z, Q, X, J, and V
These are words caught by the sun, in nets of golden wires
Scheduled rumors dance in stadiums
Less line numbering, scars and chords
Serpents in my hands
Traffic light, mixed drinks and mixed greens
Mix and burn swimwear, mix a little Goose in this juice
Your serious plans, your prudence, your moisturizer, your champagne and tigers
A little cake, dragons and lithium, comets over Corn Island
Seemingly unrelated aggression, lyric sleep defines the carpet
Endless, unsolvable meaning, acts of culture
Alligator facts and allergic reactions, trees are a logic problem
Manswers, death etiquette, party favors, party dresses at the Parthenon
Competencies, periphery, decorations disappear in the solidworks
Inflammatory diary, in Latin American emphasis, in latex
Enlarged nuchal translucency
Non-shedding dogs convert large numbers to scientific notation

Prank call this phone number
I love you, I miss you, I speak a little French, I Google you
I made a game with zombies in it and then manifested my soulmate
Manipulation under anesthesia, histrionic and hidden fields
She novelized her static and sent a postcard to Henry Purcell
A secret virus, a demure maiden, a worn path in the clouds
An amnesia prayer, a snowman's bones
Etaqualone in Bubbleland, shaky shaky, improvident
Handwriting, hatching leopard gecko eggs, red jumpsuit apparatus
Socket, cough, white wine

In comparison charts, her breathing was coherent
Use the word "coherent" in a sentence
When "chaotic" means "dictionary"
We're controlling metamaterials here
all these non-coherent falling trees
Even her footwear was famous
Heretics and heartbreak in the hereafter
He is less educated than her, less attentive
Sleep smoking, the sodium in sea salt, less studied languages and diseases
She studied the behavior of infinite sequences
the nonobservance of his Agrippa
For a heist in France, studied facial expressions, the forensics of fried chicken
Fluid mechanics, fluctuating asymmetry, joke, fever, workweek
A Venetian bestiary and its plaster of sincere interest
Trace, touch, crouch, pause, engage
When the critic cries, "Dollhouse!"
Cross-eyed palmistry, patterns, palm trees

The paper eyelashes on her astrodentist
Astronauts are particles as smooth as hoarfrost, teacups
As temperature increases pressure, the solubility of gases and solids,
volume and resistance
She wanders alone through photography
His eyes are like sparrows, like Japan or fidelity
The earth's summary, all red in explanation
Waves of ammonia among her cloudy trophies, her mattresses
She is a two-premise deductive argument, an illusionist
Her house is an illustration, her ferns fear god

Wrong conclusions autotune her head through a windshield
Dog years, cat years, gerbil years, geology
In general, what is meant by the texture of a rock or the cause of a sea breeze?
In gestures, their origins and distribution, their dynamic language dimension
What is the gesture and participation in the activity of searching for a word?
Skin overnight in antonym

Nothing of value was lost, but you know the end of this story:
the new moon blossoms and ruins, priceless, pernicious
She is patient, she is parachute, she is papering the windowpanes
She is part of the music continuum
part of the hemoglobin that binds oxygen
Hibiscus and hipbone, part of these parole conditions
Her bones are made of coral, poured out like pasture
Is Percocet on the periodic table?
Themeforest, corrupt water, atelier
This poem might be a transient madness toward advanced mathematics
This poem might be a transfer in heat between particles of a substance

This poem was written after my poem "Folio #1" as it was suggested by Google.

Devote yourself to Smallville and all the squirrels who cared for you
Astound and betray an astral projection
For example: a flower, a relational database or a letter of complaint
Metaphors, personification, hyperbole
A million little pieces of irony in his minor heart
A mistake of fact is a defense to criminal liability
What about a charity kiss for Mr. Heavenly Brainwash?
Is it a mistake to write off the Weinsteins?
Toponyms, mistaking thirst for hunger, prodigal or unfavorable
Label or negate?
Labradoodle labelmaster, acacia strain, ginger smitten
The accumulation of blood in a pleural place
Snow as a fluid within his epidermis
A map and a kiss, a mirror and a wristwatch
The crows fly like outdoor wallpaper, you are simile small
Asthenosphere, astral images darken reality
or the Athena-sphere
Heavy boots and hygiene in space
The electromagnets that get you high
Thermidor woodlands, the recurrent laryngeal nerve
Recurrence pattern is not valid
Recursive universe, split lips, spider dreams
They are a worksheet, an oracle that materializes in view
Is paranormal activity usually pink?
Literary elements, personality training, fat radishes
Favors of the moon, enchanted shooting tips
Spaceship bedding, sparklers
Use the word "sullen" in a sentence
Autism, ovulation, the zodiac of dehydration
Grease fires are signs for the unbeliever
taken for wonders on a greasy lake
How greasy ARE those potato chips?
Are born sinners true to size? Are clams alive?
Slippy, aster

Sometimes falling is an appropriate response
Sometimes for fun I hang glide on a Dorito
Sometimes form
Forms of poetry, forms of birth control
Forms are not self-subsistent substances
The carbons of our mental status
White goat machine, the lower range of human hearing
The lower right quadrant of the abdomen

Pandora in Pottery Barn
Flipping and chipping probables, Dock Ellis pitching on acid
orYANY studded leather hobo
Balaclava, bear or battleship
Mold infestations, mini bots
How do you say "house of bugs" in Spanish?
Lanterns and leveling machines
How much air is left in the lungs after expiration?
It hurts when I walk, even heaven hurts
Sparrowdark, princesspaint, fanfiction
Cluster headaches in smiling rhino theater
Do eyelashes grow back?
Easily bruised card tricks, sunlight and pronouns

Say "school" in German. Say "scrapbook" in Spanish. Say "science" in Japanese

Scaffolding, schema, her Schematic Heaven
Gutter, shades of why, beginnings are delicate times
Dragon age, draw your own great pile of leaves
Fandango dawn, grim joggers, his orbital bone
Poptropica, dromology, an example of a nonelectolyte is…
The theory of dromology interprets the world and reality as a result of velocity
Canvas gloss, cataracts in Catalan

Sometimes this poem wants to die

Women's whisper bootie, Eiffel tower knee high boot, tackling dummy
Rocketfish, rocketdog, science meat grows in a lab
Green thumbs in Greek mythology

The Easteralphabet with cutouts for your face
Ways the world could end, ways to keep pathogens out, ways guys flirt
The science of cartography is limited
Pickaxe through those expanded notation worksheets
Space holiday Japanese gum, her sparkler dims, uses for vinegar and gold
Nazi zombies have their hands on five red phones

This poem was written after my poem "Folio 2" as it was suggested by Google.

Beliefnet, plating, poisoning
Noble gas configuration burlesque
No telephone to heaven, no hands
At the Motel Bowtastic, owls burn like electric lights
Moderne boyfriend mystic spacemyth
MyVarian, MyVaporStore, MyHotComments, MyHolySpirit
My heart is a dolphin, while my hands go on a holocaust vacation
My hollow drum, my holiday burns
Papotanic multicolor text leveling/wrangling, lemony text
Lemonade mouth, Lemierre's syndrome, marine refrigeration
Proust the Squid, Marcel the Shell, pronounblocker
Fugitive Cadmatic, the cadence of Cadillacs and dinosaurs
Drinking water dreams, drosophila, dross
Laundry fields, in this Lysistrata the women want
lycophyta, whiskey wedding wrestling
In the Galileo arcade, a woman mails a puppy
In this grid of recycled words and light
taxidermied tessellations
Time machine, the clear button, the web to draw in crowds
Escape the room, where rice reacts
Sequencing the body for boys, their quadratic meats
Quassy, Quashawam, pearls, peaches, peacocks
Tea river wind, whiteuranium
In the mermaid store: her costume of ideas, chrome
Buggeryville for beginners, keep walking, beguiled, blackeyed
Dustbowl, ducksong, riddles, ballrooms adorned
Giant Girl Arrested, chicken and chatroulette, cake boss for cannibals

Bohr model, bolts, boiling point
The body's burden, its concentration and its distribution in space
Fat proof, body dysmorphic disorder, diode, dissatisfaction
Body disposal, the distribution of phosphorus, nanoparticles
Disturbia, diamonds and diazepam
Diagram a sentence like a heart

Aristotle's classification scheme is an architecture, a sentence
Diagram a sentence for me
The ascending aorta like an asteroid belt
Astromeridian, minor planets, orbital elements, fundamental catalogues
poems cadavered and puttied
Cadmium, Fenton's reaction, butterhead lettuce
Bubble letters are materials that allow heat to go through
All magic wards in the Gregorian calendar are considered harmful
Cameras take pictures of extinct animals and canonized saints most recently luminous
Mysteries in landscapes, flux factories, limestone
Robust analysis dropkicked at the National Prayer Breakfast
The theology of gout on the Marshall Islands

This poem was written after a list of Cadmium Text Series search terms as it was suggested by Google.

THOSE DARLING FEET ARE
NOT AFRAID OF ANYTHING

A store filled with shade, and then the bees said, "Oracle, oracle!"
Tranced magic, painted caves, her porcelain clothes
Willows in a blind country, protons in gold, Prometheus as your prehistoric pet
Confidentiality, carrots, cloisters, clutter ring
Indiana by degrees, byzantine
The exquisite interview, impossibly both ray and star
What if I was paid to dream about you?
I am bored as the number four
Are we Australian? Autocorrect my dyskinesia
Using the Tardos algorithm, by perseverance the snail reached the ark
The conquest of memory by the young
Pyrex was no crackpot
These are sugar-frosted prisons
Charcoal, cheddar cheese tastes like aging
Cheesy pickup lines in an annoying orange
She eats like attics, mysteries, annuals
Paprika shoes, a case of chords, and for you an exploding mango
A case of your stage stripes, stutter during treatment
Shotgun shells and Smart Water
Let's study BOTH sailors and whales
Bordeaux and grand cru, the smell of St. Elizabeth's roses
The good martyr, a black ointment made of cured olives and doves, thistle and hemp
Bare feet, starlings sun-conjured, and then submarines suddenly appear
Our sunflower hearts hulled in a photofield
How many calories are in those sutras anyway?
Seeds for flatlands, the tropics in winter
Wars that bloom around our feet
What is the cause and effect of turning her into a musical?
Hummingbirds for Hume were the resemblance of contiguity and causation
Everywhere, humanscale freedom chairs are dead or mating in New York

Humans can lick too, corrupted by body temperature, coral reefs
Cormorants in the foundling hospital
Are the Straits of Magellan ever fuchsia?
Strappy guava, strawberry panic, winter as seen on TV
A complete thematic unit: plants vs. zombies
Photoautotrophs, a ruby wedding with thorns
Rift in Roseland, anatomy afterwinters as a symbol
Remember that both cheerleaders and war criminals start fires
Bless a blurred man and his acid soils
Fetuses in jars that look both presidential and unfinished
A fig walked into a bar for a kiss
Treeman disease, tree marriage, assault ship
Is the size of Japan the same size as a queen bed?
Charts made of silk galaxy tabs, drawn by a bellows mender
Angel diction in modern usage = "String, string!"
Stand an egg on end, bamboo fun, bamboozle prom
Fisheye bite alert with elastic, fishcharm, strike indicator
Polyvore, give me those linen codes before I sleep
Persistence, persimmons, poppies and cats' eyes
surround a lagoon of bibles
The city newly sleeved in aluminum

*This poem was written after a list of presents Bernadette Mayer wanted for her birthday in 2011
as it was suggested by Google.*

THIS IS A CHEEZBURGER DREAM
SPEECH DRESS UP

I love the way you lie on Danger Jesus
Restless spoilers, your machine embroidery has been…
Well, nut crusted halibut, Batman
Straightening balm, a concordance of symptoms, her glowdark perfume
I accept the rising as you offered it to me, infiltrated with salmon
teahen theories, the deluxe mirage, word vampires

Too much summary, too much analysis, too much meaning to paraphrase

I throw my hands up in the air sometimes and turn polar bears white
Instead of crying or being late, I try on these sentences
Sugar sunsets and a separate unfortunate event
Sincerity in shards, signature-based counter methods
or a significant example of Petula Clark
It's your birthday or your gallbladder acts up or the bottoms of your feet turn yellow
These are your superpowers and you must know how to use them
Awkward family photos in a chapel of foxes
The world in French means "oystervampire"
Wear your awareness bracelets
Maybe you've been booed in a beautiful Korean drama
Maybe you ran from bubble shooters in the mullet latitudes
Don't you think it's a little weird that I've got to ask you twice?
Infinity fishing, I fight dragons
You can find inmates in prison for free at Find-A-Grave
My head hurts when I cough, my head never stops shedding and peeling
My head needs a skin shield, my head is a giant egg
My head on your chest caving in
No collar fish jigs, tartanic
He sailed around Ireland in a fridge
leaving behind wax drippings in the shape of an angel
I'm ankle deep in your oceans, your opinion journals

Look at the way that vehicle is affixed to the word "heaven"
My clock has tremors, achievement smells like mildew
My hair makes me look fat, my jaw pops when I chew
Speculative moths in ruin, I swell and snap
Aunt Jennifer's tigers and their gorgonzola stare
A shot at history with tequila or a fume of sighs
A mouse could fit under your sternum…if it was open
Shattered snooze, light apparently drowns
Was he attacked by tarpon? Did he die near cairns?
You are the only exception, and soon there was darkness and deserts
We worship gangs of losers
We are grammar and I approve this message
Are funeral expenses tax deductible?
Ferrets, fingerprints, fever blisters
Bend your arms to look like wings
Spirit animal spinal team, piano anatomy, Chinese flowers
Like a Tiki village or a talking god, a talking muffin, a talking pumpkin
Defensive phone holster
We just lost the moon where the patellar ligament attaches
Dandelion dust in the air like dreaming backwards
Decimals dissolve into poinsettias
Disco lemonade dissolves like meaning
The location of wishes in the golden sun
Released rituals, incantations
The day before disclosure, we've managed to eliminate the stars
Blindness blooms like blessings
Kansas bleeds like a pair of bleached jeans, black apples
You can camp on Montauk, or drive in Florida, or smoke in Hawaii

In this underwater battle: it's tiger leech vs. crab

I am not a human being, I've got Barry Manilow disease
Puppet lyrics, number one fan, footnote generator
Huckleberry redeemer, gummy bear, lyric angel, god
Can your baby read this coupon?
I am a proofreading machine with actual saliva
Do you hunt deer in posted places?
Do you hunt like a girl? Do you hunt Canada?

What is your legal right after someone punches you?
Your legs shake, your dreams fall in love with you
Princess poem, are mermaids Christian?
Are Mormons real? Are mushrooms also monsters?
Are my ears on straight? Are my pearls real?
Palace Solitaire, so are we going to kiss or not?
Is my license suspended, are my legs supposed to jiggle?
Has my light wasted energy with heat?
Limabean bushpole, too bright for my aquarium
Lime orange tree book won't fruit
Jell-O salad disease, the length of tea
The pressure of water in lyric, travertine
Cherry festival weather
Vulnerability schema, broadcast yourself
You been booed in my heart
You're a touch overrated, a tool shed rental
You're a tool to measure humidity, to remove spiral wire
A slang to measure mass
You work with chains and you must have been high
Evanescent embroidery eclipsed
You enjoy myself, and now you've entered into an expression with no value
The bloody Hürtgen forest, measurements to determine body shape
Map coordinates, arrogant hockey worms
Deerpants, dead fish market, the Deadman's Bible
Delicate determinism with detached retina
Detailed character list , dragon song, pheasant tail feather, muscle,
Barely breathing and shaped like a house: the signs that someone is lying
Side ponytails, the pathology of goal theory
I am a pineapple in French, I am picky, a basket-shaped October
What value is a simple stain?
Wisteria skin poisoning, straggle daisy

Are there any trillionaires? Without eyes?
Are the seasons capitalized?
Blow a raspberry in the fishing guild bank, blow an egg out of its shell
Blow across the back of a jackknife

Acrylic fish Christmas ornaments
This sentence does not exist
Will this sentence ruin or save your life?
I contain two errors, and the sequence is not important
This sentence contains all words starting with the letter N
Red ferns worship telepathic Châteauneuf-du-Pape 2007
Who was eliminated from the stars?

This poem was written after my poem "Inadequate Stovetop Remix" as it was suggested by Google.

MICROTONAL ACCIDENTAL FONT

A variable that is manipulated by the scientist in an experiment
Structural adaptations that equal character
A variation on the powers of 10, or for the word "sleep"
Let's swap veins
The calculus in a Korean folk song or a Shaker melody
Kernel sentences informed by Rilke, Hayden, Paganini, Levertov
Musical chairs, missionaries, mac n' cheese, mimosas
Servitude to moonlight and the morality of rain
Monogamy interpolated, my monolingual fears
Formula closure, mono sets, quantile and convex functions
Monologue, monotype, the likelihood ratio for love
Anthropologists are participant observers, revelators
The autobiography is also an alphabet game
Martyrology, dust canters, horseradish, cloudy eye
Leap over your own meals
Horse chestnut extract prancing, funny or die
Ladybugs, the ground folds up with meaning, flaxfault
From pimp stick to pulpit, memory foam remembers
The shattered sun hoards artifacts, we celebrate islands
The ascent of money as a character in world history
Ascetic glitches, ascension packs a punch wrapped in tissue paper
Easter Egg Island golf course, zombie tourism

Are we really protected from accidental deletion?

Even the flowers these days are professional
Remember that time when that fat man was dropped?
Thatched, that free thing softly under Christmas
Fountain texting, a thesaurus cracks open in the wrong hands
Our Atlantic senses fail, that intolerable gloss
That skinny Scottish mist, the sea burns with forgetting
in codeine seas, the grasslike uncertainty in sea monkeys

Glide density, dislocation models crystal grain boundaries
The motion in metals, in brittle fracture
The sheer force of a reckless bureaucracy
Arcane prankster munchies, aromatherapy as a substitute or London
The belly becomes the crib, a basket of sun
Lyrics hang around your neck, your handwriting has no tears in it
All arms around you, Halloween Alaska
Inkheart, godfont, pleated with Pleaides, skindex
Poppies know the pleasure of being robbed, of flinching
An invaded suffering, obscurity, open water
Please touch my museum, our hands are oracles
In operant conditioning an organism learns
Skin splitting open, the structure of infection
A template of classes, her cirrus dress
The sun warms the earth by convection
Constellations by constructivism
Demotivational, decorations darken a room, demonoid
Breast cancer defines its own accessibility
Why isn't there a love defibrillator? Insanity benefits technology
Define "irony." Define "leadership." Define "culture"
The defenestration of this poem in relation to others
The midline of the body, paper buttons, plateaus
Pies and Thighs, Crimecraft is next to the Piercing Pagoda
Cartilage or orchid, zombie spacecraft or wasting syndrome
Does god choke on these situations?
Text citations for "Silence: the Musical"
Voodoo and the brain, loss is a voice recognition system
Tangled news of a distant ascension
Which voices are never used in cantatas?
Arousal theory, a family of words, eyelashes both positive and false
Dichotomy in falsetto, prophets in pretense and forensics
Feathering her fear of long words are:
clowns, heights, god, death, failure, snakes, intimacy, plastic bags, plane crashes
Summoning small continents, backsplash burn-treatments, seabelly treasures
the speed of thought, the space taken up by a window
When a spirit takes over your body
Overspiritualizing over spilled milk, a moonless heartbreak

her spiral curls, how to cross over spirits, the light over Norway
Spirit jailbreak, grace wasted on excess capacity, slanted
Lamentation an idiom for fitted sheets, fortune cookies, retraction
Turtled to death, the bejesus twist, smokewagon
Threadless, a foreign object circulates in the blood
Fish an animal, fox a dog, frog a reptile, fetus a person
Double spaced food poisoning, the structure of this space
Avalanche, indigo directions, how wind is a discography
a funeral of hearts, cypress cognates, crooked vultures
The pleasure of objectification is an invalid
The chanterelles have changed their address

This poem was written after my poem "Microtones" as it was suggested by Google

We ingest our definitions
Hand sanitizer, orange mold, rust, bath salts
Video iodine Vaseline, snake venom
There are traces of sulfur in his saliva
Silica gel dessicant
What happens when you inject silicone into dogs or babies?
Oh Barcelona, the Carolinas breathe like memory
The sky is sienna with dust in a polaroid spring
Hold your breath in Spanish
A dress made of pollen
Arabidopsis, a genomic and transcriptive view
Dead Island, at the disability market
An android eclipse destroyed Brooklyn

An algorithm for selecting objects
An algorithm for the binary split search
An algorithm that computes the kth smallest
An algorithm for suffix stripping

An allergy to allegiance, this is an American haunting
Allow for doubtful accounts
an origami burlesque maze, substitute berries for wood
Add leaves to her love fire
Definitions on the tongue, on the liver, on the skin
Scarlet tactics, Scrabble cheat, scalloped
She is scolded by the definitions around her
Plug in the electric zoo, but protect the poets
Things are far from okay

How do you play piano in Japanese?
Follow these invented instructions

Just where is the equipment for translation located?
Witch hazel is just within temptation

A pale horse made out of silk stockings
Shells tatting in a pocket, remove fluid from the lungs
To build a fire is not out of the question
To be lost like a synonym, longing always for morale
Lionpit/snowyday, a pile of days in a Pilsner glass
We are happy to be paid in cookies
A pile of crowns stuffed in a pillowcase for Basquiat
The wind heaped shoes at the bottom of the stairs
Pileated woodpeckers or a pile of lemons?
Shame soots out secrets, our miserable sediments
Sequential types, sharks can dance with travel
A slanting device clothed as an explanation
A slogan for mercury, a rain-whispered alphabet
Sugar flowers drive through your Spanish
Do your emergency plans include sugar cookies AND parchment?
Rags and doves piled up like palindromes
Cat fur, cake pops, carpet stain removal, hot tub guys, noise-canceling headphones
She's in texture therapy
If it scares squirrels, does it also help you sleep?
Did I pluck you from the present tense?
Perfect skin and perfect pitch
How to attain that panic?
Ponies overdose on bridal showers in the biblical sense

This quintessential dust moves like bees
Yeti Sasquatch Annihilates Crab Zombie
Does Christ really need grammar? The desert overrides him
Never clean your gutters again
in your "never say never" clothes
At the paintball clinic, summarize this pail of air
Say I'm hung up on gravity
Say it once, glass pear

Outrageous Waikiki, at sea a reef of libertarians
This is what happens when saints go machine in the séance cinema
The shadows on her skin encased in ice
She's a one-eyed doll
Evening paints a long taut rope affixed to a post
Pandemic narrow grasses, nascent satellite, patterns of string
This trap is always complicated and sunny
Sugarfluff fades, casts crowns
Sleep no more! Slimebasketball all the time in this stainless cherry heaven
Furious idioms, songwater, ghosts, storm doors
Sipeliculas, splash and splinter, the unreleased somnambulist
The valves of her attention, cloverfields, the systems read you
The new backwards kissed me and the clouds opened

*This poem was written after an anagram poem for Leslie Scalapino by Lynn Behrendt
as it was suggested by Google.*

DOGTOOTH IN A DREAM VINEYARD, WHITESTONE

Shock arrives in slow motion
What are a dog's inspirational quotes, anyway?
Do they flush positive ions of their meaning?
She found that without a spacesuit, it was impossible to cry
Her interspinous interiors
It's always 1982 in the dark, your face like a black ops Ibiza
The space in a relationship should be about the size of a poem
In pursuit of tea in plain sight, are you a Kiwisaver or a Kiwispender?
What else could you be?
This is a kitchen to thwart writer's block
Kite ova, a kitten for Hitler, a kitten kills, a kitten a day calendar
Bronxville manifesto: where hairspray smells like falling in love
The crab and its relatives or a bronze clown statue story
The closed treatment of common fractures
Stomata disadvantages, vinyl lettering labels the state of Virginia
Vacuole ashfield asylum quotes seas like verbs
Crow tears taste like ginger, they are tranquil ashtrays those birds
Traffic lights and their meanings, light squared
An abundance of Katherines abstracted
That an abstract noun cannot name a firecracker is an abscessed idea
An absence so great and spontaneous it is an evidence of light
Seizures color in the margins of her notes for school
Baby teeth, Barr bodies, darker than air, the herpes hereafter
Peeling eggs and the skin on her feet skins us
Gorgonite eyes begin to glow
To grow reefs, there has to be some following
Where are the lyrics to her spacesuit?
I want something different and blue to eat
There's something terribly enthralling about the exercise of influence
or a woman with a gun in a noodle shop, or a tulip palisade
or a bowling ball aimed at a clarinet

Spinning in snow, Shrinky Dinks, an eel bride bamboozled
Stuffed with Love, a Taxidermy Emporium
where god dropped the paint bucket, WoWhead
Winter squash, whales, plush waffles
Landfill: the Movie
The deferred ocean or a dollhouse full of text
Escapist, expendable as an event in the rain
Crossfire handbag, evening crosses print
Licking screen, we are panic prone in the needle park

This poem was written after my poem "Dogs in Space – Remix" as it was suggested by Google.

I wasn't thinking about Futurestan, when the noon sun
was directly overhead at the equator and the noodles were uncooked
Noonday demons are an atlas of depression
She's got noon tattooed in wedding wine text
You can wear my shirt, my eyelash extensions, my mollusks, my annelids
Minor arcana supplement terrain features
A subminor solar fort is one definition of ascension
A worn path, cloudadjacent, a lack of color stocked with 500 fish
We are protected from receiving the wind
over a lake of beer for god
Sleeping children, dead languages, streambed alteration ragepond
A lake full of wolf eyes is a form of grammar
Books, smoke, reckless pride, balloons, trampoline ghosts
Cupcake text your glory chords as hatecargo
The little surprises in liquid sodium
A bible made of light, lime curd and liquor
Withdraw beneath an algebra maple
Linen drawings at fingernail latitudes, or am I just an abbreviated symmetry?
A few dollars combined with a man who makes potions is a wolf nightmare
a beautiful lack, a night of neglect, a noiseless patient spider
A sun angle calculator or an ornament savior
The singular plural will try to kill you
Singularity theorems, is your new red skull a game, a moon god?
On the skin brown plains, the sendusing field configuration value is invalid
Her senile and delinquent prayers are seamless
Confetti lamps, rosemary, varnish ingredients
Her Mercedes a flat ginger
After an oyster parade, mermaid remains washed up on the beach
Remorse Code, Sermon Spice, sleep in the absence of photography
When your shoes are dated by violence, French horror falls out of your sleeves
The slightest whim-adjusting slippers, neonatal gold
Indian genesis tree lyric, the state of matter at room temperature
Isotopes and fish density, delectation
I wish you'd snore more like a fat and drunk smoker
The romanticism in Roman numerals

Totem Lake taped and gorgeous away from farms, crosswords, cardigans
Idiomatic bed images, pig earth, their lips mimic grammar
Faced lined with sand, mousekeeping, metallic
Nylons, pizza, lactose, starch, monomania
She had an omenectomy for clarity, yet they continue to read her like Cinderella
They should cage lead singers at night
as they reminisce and collapse over their instruments
Artists smell like honey, foxes and heartbeats
In Monstercockland, weddings accessorize the rain
Facts blow across this ocean, misnumbered
Simmer her in her shimmer lipstick
When is the mid-season miracle sale?
What if Memphis-bleak merchant ships were girlicious?
Was Thomas Jefferson also a Thai prostitute?
American dream therapy, or a god that never goes outdoors
A room with no floor, the shutters blow in, filled with toys, lyrics and light switches
Rectangle a square, rabbit a rodent, rose a monocot
One humid perspective is that the moon landing is blue tonight
River chattel, is leopard print stronger than chemotherapy?
How many calories are in the south of France?
Our skeletal structures follow a nuclear reaction
Thieving guide, valence shell, legs like twigs
Fables and masterpieces barely done by simple machines
Lessons learned from geese on bullying
Eye clothing, a nostalgia for nose bleeds, the awe in thank you notes
Moonsoup, moons named after gods and Shakespearean characters
What's a noun that starts with the letter U? Understanding is uniform and uncountable
Lug nuts and ligaments, animal facts as pets and loss
Pearls that look like an Arctic attack, and then a Leonid meteor explodes
Relics of prayer float in the sky, relic hoarders
Sacramentary in your immortality suit, in the red jaws of your French palace
Origin wallpapers over pleasure
Losslessness joins decomposition in celandine
Your nausea, your appetite, the effects of alcohol, your stretchmarks
The appearance of your scars remove all doubt from reels of dreams unrolled

This poem was written after my poem "When the Noon Wears Ermine" as it was suggested by Google.

SHE WAS AN INVENTED FORM OF LOVE

Her biceps were both interactive and saved by rock and roll
Her space holiday was a like a copper wire lisp
Her Oklahoma had lucky pretty eyes
wore an organza made of oil and oval shaped screams
The mirrors rattled
Her profile roamed
The halls were ultra simple
She laughed by proxy
Her laundry fields were filled with lamb-red meat
She bought her lacrimal bones over the counter
She was born with a lyric gland
Caviar dream font, Caviarteria
She had an affair with codfish and ash, with Warsaw avocados, with cigarette appetizers pumped with vodka
And also the trees as such
She could use the word "avarice" in a sentence
She was a totem to prodigality and covetousness
She knew that avarice cannot synchronize with cartoons
She can't tell the difference between Caravaggio and caramelized onions
Her sea salt is gluten free and from Montana
She was an invented candy of illuminati informed intentions
Her hands were rescued by an oracle
She makes casseroles out of war
She has a continuous lean toward miracles like a carat of gold
Her camels, her china, her facts diagrammed
She fishes in financial Egypts, her pool is filled with caramel
Christ in school prayer with cheese please
She is capitalized in cat-like tread
She is a cleverbot, an international rose celebration
She makes the saints run to windows, head belly up to the sky
She sailed accountancy through bloody seas
She is more cowbell than half marathon

Her volatility awaits the treasure market
She has vivid dreams in Port of Spain
She will be remembered for giving in
She wonders if texturizers are better than relaxers?
Which is better, beer or god?
She conducts her relationships in quotes
She is an emissary to relic castles
Her jacket is celestial
Her body is carved out of sandwiches and crushed Portland
She plays rabbit babysitting and rabbit dress up
She sings coffee songs and hangs thermal-lined curtains
She is a confusing summary of no homework and cracked bones
There is poverty behind every crime, and crime behind every fortune
Chicken meat cheerleading, a voice full of money
Vanished grace, she is a bureau of adjustments
The amount of surface runoff increases the amount of light that enters the eye
filtering a violent and flammable world
Poets phone the abyss, reclusive
Someone made her out of reclaimed lumber, storm horses, tailhooks
"You can build your own malice," she said
Her vodka vocabulary over glaciers, stochastic
She has Stockholm syndrome and a stocked pantry
She practices extreme etiquette
Her movements echo with ecclesiastic approval
She was made from scratch
She is clairvoyant, sleeps late and snores
She points her Claddagh ring at people
Her clavichord rivals a crock pot
She was a milk experiment in Maine and an oral history
She wonders what an orange traffic sign means
Her oracle bone was wrapped in white paper
She was also an oracle of modernism in ancient Rome
Her planting instructions involved the Super Bowl
She went to the cemetery where Al Jolson was buried
Her root cellar is filled with camel spiders
She is an orange mild cigarette
She is entirety in its simplest form

The velvet grip of her vein idiom, she is structured like cilia
She orchestrates Ravel like an Olympic horse
Hers is an aspen-feathered dress
Her verbs are metaphors for freedom
She is an adaptation in bats
When an object freely falls it is an imperfect actor on the stage
She is an orienting response
Nest myth, fabric, symbol, birdhouse
Her address is a bird park
Tiger informally, orange month oil or blue jay egg
She is an aquamarine herbicide
The mummies in her coat are so warm, they're on fire
She formed the "I Am Here" coalition
Coalesce, clamshell buckets, narratology
She wants a meaningful life filled with new architecture
She is cloud agnostic
Her clover necklaces a clown fish, clover grows in her grasses
Grass grows over her vibrating concrete
Her viability replicates definitions
She is in a nondividing state, a laboratory manual
Reed mystery triptych, a whorehouse quintet
Keith Richards is her essay in human understanding

This poem was written after my poem "Her Lilac Ovals Roam" as it was suggested by Google.

Side lengths her sparrowed Japans
Tetrahedron wolfram Mathworld
Tell all the truth but slant it with analysis
Chicken heads, be quiet
Cheetah Girls, say all the cheeses in alphabetical order
This is a cherry blossom blacklist manifesto
The inspirational quotes in infomercials are like dancers adjusting their slippers
North American birds telegram their touring caravans
In a milliyet, what is the meaning of a tossed salad?
The islets of Langerhans or Stiletto Spy School
Apiaries, morphlings, moisture meter, instant whitening
Morning slang in translation's ginger, an omission paradise
Swim school, tiger beetles, leechking
Lattice field lyrics, liturgical as a little Vassar
She's got a touch of frost called "panic," and is a total waste of makeup
Acoustic taboo summary, a fault tolerant book
A madrigal suspended like a secular god in a sunbeam
Polyphonic prayer, a slim optical slot
His marriage was new every morning, at the mercy of his money cologne
This is a metadescription of Maryland
Her mouth had subtitles, Sweeneybloomed
Chinese zodiac, chisel-couture, a violet and lemon Navy wedding
Rust remover, crab grass preventer
They are dressed ideally for a revolution
Agnostic and theistic Satanism, theists gone wild
Does god exist in the encyclopedia?
Their cowgirl lives for grammar, their list-buried lives
Seahorses say goodbye in different languages
An ideological oddity annoyed by forever
Those seen dancing were followed by footnotes, abbreviated kingdoms
Fangraph hands lean wisely on great forces like parasites and supernovas
Anemones hosting and licking superfruit

What is the pronunciation of "sleeping sickness?"
Steal shade, slick deals for SleepNoMore, Sleet helmet
Slope intercepts form in pleated sheets
Chew bubble gum as the winners go by in their cheap perfumes
Our chemical image of the invisible, the chemise she wore at her execution
in henna seduction
Are you afraid of a dark where lap giraffes are real?
Are mermaids funny or evil or brittle?
A crowd in a microwave, where snow can lead to apples and ivy
An arrangement to defraud definition in a sorrow walkthrough
Yeah, yeah, yeah
Fun, fun, fun
Shell variables tease you with applescript
Collect souls in this sentence and their selective mutism
Perfection makes her look thinner
What do they wear in Madagascar? What do Situationists wear?
Chinese lanterns, electronic cigarettes, dead symphonies
Turns out the world has a crush on the integral solace of sorrow
The physics of secrets, is the world going to end on Saturday?
Are rocks gay? Mistletoe cancer, piano wire
A chemistry student explains hell as an artist + a lot of fizz
A chemist was given four unidentified wishes to strengthen a mixture:
emblems + everyone's got a random engine
everything started to fall apart + her etcetera creams

This poem was written after my poem "His Isosceles Tell-All" as it was suggested by Google.

Pictures of Jesus with bedbugs resized to frame
What is your strategy for spotting the difference between sky sports?
Sequences segmentation, an unoptimized reading of the spine
What are the properties of real numbers?
Logic is the clay with which we were created
Out come the wolves of grammar
Probability, her filters were not enabled
Flagstone discipline, Fiestaware in the Fidelity Museum
Magnetic examples marked with an asterisk
The Mapplethorpe super-class disappears
surrounded by hibernating lyrics, mapped but not known
Buttermilk channels buttercream frosting

How do you say "but I'm a better cheerleader than you" in Spanish?

What not to put in the septic tank
Sunrise over the memory of Google
September allows structure to turn into light
Separation anxiety in dogs, separate colors when doing laundry
Why do colors separate in chromatography?
Science splashed on a magazine
Diamond shine lip gloss just outside of the human heart
The diagonalization of a latex dress
She is a striping machine
The frayed sunlight is too fond of books
A character trait informed by limestone
Does the creator play typing games?

Antipsychotics
Closing costs
Situational Chinese foods

A theme in a long story about a red toy
A granule in the photosphere is the size of uselessness
An unidentified flying chicken, bodies, objects, plant parts improvise
Imperialism is an impossible game, as are domestications
An introverted intuition, irreducibly diagonally dominant
The heartbeat is irreversible, a holy experience in New Jersey
When a body lies on a frictionless surface
overgrown, overweight, overgrazing
Tenderness is a theorem proof in Cupid's cocoon
Property has the greatest entropy, weeks like bad massages
How long have I been a mother to myself?
Malignancy legends, a strange cake book, vesperbuild

He invented the question mark
He invented the clothes dryer
He invented lying

The inverted forest of her imperious condescension, her immortality
Imagine swimming in heaps of narrative and then he kissed me
Confidence intervals hinge, symbols burn like dollars
He was 70 degrees, all the weather in heaven
He was so ugly that everybody died and he never had a girlfriend
Was someone just kissing me?
Add Jell-O and say something adorable to your boyfriend
Analyze a daffodil murder
Sheet music may have difficulty showing emotion
Charitable and piteous, her empress name
Her skin reviews him
They liked each other like a quiz
Lives like apostrophes, as if pixels married
Tamer animals, butter roses
Married like old machines, created romantic images
Idiomatic preaching for children
Over 30 years combined experience in acne
A bomb shelter divorce, stars hang in the night like housewives

Giants reminisce over you

Let's have some expendable wrong fun
singing for England like sick animals

Similarity colonies
Disorganized attachment
Red wings
Buttonhole
Blood clot
Brain stem
Glass bedding
Rain
Rice paper
Bone marrow
Nail polish
Infant sorrow
Underbite
Unexplained crying

In which quadrilateral are the diagonals always congruent?

Ocean octaves, yam haze, solidworks
Worm apocalypse, family poems are futile devices
The worms have eaten the puppies
Terminology

Where is my refund in heaven?
Refraction, variability, abundance
exorcisms and certain supplications
Of each particular thing ask what it is in itself
Ultra nostalgia liquid flavoring
Threadless cups of tea, an investigation into magic numbers
Identical fatigue mechanisms like the 1994 biography of Calvin Klein
Masses of stars along uniform book lengths
Sizzle tans the size of Japan
A bushmaster reels in gold from the Chinese zodiac

This poem was written after my poem "Folio #23" as it was suggested by Google.

IN A GOLF GALAXY

The periodic table or the moon on the ocean floor?
The oblivion on Oregon beaches:
One side oxidized, one side silver
His hand a symbol or a
Nova Scotia tree movie or a
hydrangea wine cluster
Can you identify holly in conservatories and vineyards?
Andy Goldsworthy and his oak leaf holes
Absence rests in lyrics, a template for galore
Gold skeleton leaves, Sasaki Gold Leaves
Her sarcophagus sandals traded for salt
A sailfin bracelet and a gramophone in Malta
A sailor moon in Saigon
where her name was a hand-me-down
Her lips as ghost cherries, shore weeds
Girls like retrievers or prisms or playwrights
The bell tolls for dummies
She was a sanctuary to conquerors
Charmed and alone, she sleeps by number
What are the symptoms of New York?
She hibernates in weight loss
I tell you I'm not going and I'm out of gum
Can you impersonate Clark Gable or an improvised explosive device?
He is a cartoon of imperialism
Imageshack trilemma: true or false?
You're a brave little toaster
Thrush market, an air-conditioned bible, rubyeyes
A gold threaded dress summary
Cypress, thimble, thong
Is gold the new pink? Mineral theater, next bubble
She is rich with coupons
A leg and foot pop out of the body
Arteries drawn on the outside, vines bursting behind her knees

Butcher's broom and butane and Bulbapedia
But for me it was Tuesday
There were martinis of meaning
This poem might have an alternate ending
Rainbow blindness without you, see-through lyrics
Thoughts of woods and supermarkets
Your words are losing weight for no reason
Ozone funhouse, the galaxytail of a ghetto Eden
Swim in air, swing the mornings around your psychiatric treatment
A garden of collectibles
In the golden age of piracy, how was "pirate" spelled?
Goddamn refrigerator, an analysis of dust and harmony in Cocteau
Light-o-rama, the blinking battery light on our evening
On this day, god wants to know why, in 1987, nothing happened
Thistle, this is why you're fat: because the stars won't go out if you slap them
This sadness has no mayonnaise, and this sandwich will never end
This salad is hilarious and is not taxable in Pennsylvania
Flush, slope tectonics off Louisiana, slave slush Himalayan
The Mondays in our hearts, our souls cough up stars
I haunt the halls of medicine at night, the discography in your dress
Enormous wings, shellpoems of the Galapagos, the names of old ships
What if PayPal delivered the atomic bomb, or the sun got its energy from this poem?
I'm pretty sure glitter could stop the war. It's a glinty religion
Glassfish, drive through rage, all your pain is greatly appreciated

BTW - This is a would-you-go-out-with-me poem
Go out and make disciples and then make dinner
where the blacktop ends and the campfires start, where the shadows edge out the cornfields
Dreams seek verbs, optics, flannel plains
The axis of awesome, the axial skeleton contains extensionality
Euclidean geometry, maximum entropy
Read the landscape according to probability, as a series of well-ordered mistakes
Wandermoon, wanderful, wandering tongue rash
The king of limbs in the key of awesome
Metals panic an alchemist. A field calculates its own mercy
Sequences of shades in shattered sun, a bottle full of distress
Polka Dot Bikini Girl, I swear our veins are infinite
She is raven with thank-yous

That light can undergo interference is evidence of brilliance
A store without a name, how to bring light into a basement
That never happened to Jesus
I never felt a wound filled with this light
I'm never going to leave this bed
Superunknown, a blue storm searches the book of forgetfulness for its fish
When the sea of Iwami is fully clothed
The sea floor is constantly shrinking to a foam motel
Fencibles, fever analysis, shredders, anesthesia
Christ's Twitter button
Wiles wash over wisdom school
A plague aloft with symbols
You painted yourself in lyrics and parked like a jackass

This poem was written after the George Oppen poem "Gold on Oak Leaves" as it was suggested by Google.

Sentences and synonyms, farmed crumbs, Jellicent
Jupiter juice, a tornado of fabric
Severally liable, a jointless bone in the body
Gaussian random variables, then continue these random variables
Her goodness was concave
Create a graph that involves cream cheese frosting
it's meaning is edible
Blindness tests, object permanence
The Dresden Dolls sing a break-up song
The formidable joy in a June owl city

Sequential things in a Google search dropdown box under the letter J:

Jews killed in the Holocaust
Jersey Shore
Jesus

Jellyfish play cards in Crap Town
The Opal of the Month Club, jelly on this hot god
Green jelly obeys the cow god, literally
Name one object in space that starts with the letter K and connotes devotion and desire
Found objects traded on the silk road, translucent and triangle-shaped
A levitation trick, Hollywood fused with war
Idlebrain at the Idle Hands Bar
How is energy gathered or created? The light seems to bleed in an aquarium
Addicting games, a doll house full of text
I'd like to find a doll I can marry
Summarize the garden, instant noodles in French
How do you say "cake" in Arabic? Or "cypress box?"
A doll in a jar, a bento box, skinwind dropout
How many ounces in a jigger?
In a domestic partnership, nonpolar covalent bonds form a jitney elopement

The rain covers bees with its interest
The soap burns with her mistakes, tiny ghosts in Lilly Pulitzer dresses

Edible arrangement rings, the Medusa stage reproduces
Super bass grenades roll deep into fireworks

Even the coral dreams of you

Greypurple, she is red with morale, with ivory and indigo iris
Icicle blue paint shimmers almost without color
She's got jazz hair in bloom, icily regular but splendidly null
Jonquils tan their guitars, their blonde Venus Helen dresses
Marrowed harmonies, he is her bone daddy
Birdsong, please fill out this injured spouse form
Clearly, she was injected with praying mantis DNA
Bleach poisons a lyric, lidocaine love leprosy
Megalomaniac philosopher-king libel tourism
Blue eyes, black wings, bright skies
Little Miss Obvious breathes on glass, kisses like this
Backstop netting, his and her hair, his bedtime body language
His beloved pet Sleep, Belgium bulged with healing properties
At the Belly Burst Animal Hospital
bewilderment ran through his veins like a caffeine project
Black tea beads, broken orange, brides in agnostic complicity
Boundless Ashgate said, "Where can I get a hot tub, you braille playboy?"
What if Juliet threw furniture off the balcony?
A baconalia on a heart- shaped beach
For all those sleeping, a few dollars more
Brother velvet revolver, bronze alloy, a rabid banana
Is a rabbit truly the king of ghosts?

This poem was written after my poem "Jollity Jointly" as it was suggested by Google.

I'm bored or on a boat
or, I'm not going to write you a love song and I'm not in a plastic bag
Placebo, without you I'm nothing
I'm not your boyfriend or your skin
Nothing and everything lyrics red
I'm not your burn notice, your toxic holiday
Forgive your enemies because it annoys them so much
You deserve nothing and I hope you get less
I want to do nothing and call it something
What weighs nothing and can be seen?
Town and country, macaroni and cheese, Turks and Caicos
Corks, asparagus, lemons, cancer
Where do reindeer live and can they really fly?
Now that I'm finally in Madrid, I can think
Do fish have ears and can they hear?
Enzymes are proteins and can therefore be deactivated
All I can think about is getting you home
and can the liver repair itself?
Thunder without lightening is like a prescribed medication
Start a sentence with Neverland
Kiss a neverwinter Pawn Star
Ghost a source volume
Chase pavement, buckle up or eat glass, wake up or eat sushi
Pope or Mussolini, make it or break it, funny or die
I embellish events because I love you not knowing why or even from where
Wonder Woman was captured repeatedly by some really sad optical poems
The Absence Band is not really sincere
Since I'm not your everything, I've decided to be the air in a Christmas play
Since I'm the best, I walk with extra gestures
in this absence tablature
The Absolut Vodka diet and hip hop abs
Absence: the Store for Lovers
Smells that repel mosquitos, cats that looks like Hitler, cows that can jump

or bees that live in the ground
Jesus is the inspiration for my medical weight loss
Why does the center of an LED light look yellow?
What the is longest name of a lake in Massachusetts?
Lake rumors, trout, boat propellers
I am a dollar sign and you are a number
You are a tourist, a bomb, a bone marrow match
We are a box of crayons
I fall through your clouds
Because I'm the vampire, that's why

Clouded leopard: noctilucent and acrylic
Negative staph in cascade, in duck blood
Can't you see you're fading?
Her bones surf somnolence
Name an activity with a test you must pass before doing
Objects must be smart, borrowed rainbows
Give me an example of an investigative project in chemistry
How did Copernicus explain the retrograde motion of the planets?
What is something you wear that starts with an M?
She flirts in French about the value of coins

You're killing me with snails
You're my loveprize
This is my favorite highway
Mathmaticious minds make industrial smog
Birds act like definition
Gestures migrate across continents
A better life, a blue whale, a brief history, a bicultural experience
A bomb brushed red in his trustworthy screaming
Canticle, cantata, Korean gummy bears
A bridge which may be raised to prevent access
without warning, with burning will collapse in 17 minutes
A parabolic arch with a flag and a red X
Toothpicks, lovelox, a sluice, a deadly extreme
Falsework, flourish bedding
Flutter flat minor in a flood of paper, floral, fluent

Minor dramatic, a flask containing molecules of gas
Flagella, watch it backwards: your season to be blessed

You're a storm that fell through my life, the sound of animals fighting
In the relationship house, a cloudgarden
Risperdal, risottoteria, fawnball
Runetotem, a rose is a ruined red record
from a radio engine to a photon wing
a radical experiment in empathy
A radio is also a walking man with predictive guts

You're the truth, I'm not
The Trentonian grass, chaste in trillionaire skins
All of the gin joints in the world
Of a river in Italian, in river idiom
The sky is a body of water and
I am old cowhand anteater organizing junkie
An open ended ocean, an obscure signal, an aviary
The rock says "Happy Birthday" in salt structure
Roasting remedies, welcome to my heart in French
You're a virgin who can't drive
You're a cantaloupe, a cinema cigarette
You're a criminal as long as you're mine
You're a crucial aspect of synchrony
You're a crucifixion narrative, a grief factory
Valiance, teleportation, devastation, winged dominance
Serum enchanted weapons
Razor ice, cinder glacier
or rather grammar, root words
What happens to Caesar after the third offering of the crown?
Romanticism toward the third of May, his charm of the week
She is third eye blind
Intercept the occipital nerve, the fourth heart sound
Sedative hypnotics and dentistry
I'm somewhere where I don't know where I am
I'm something, stupid DO me
What's something smart to say about math? Or post on FB? Or say to a girl?

The small orange of your back, ornamental trees grow out of office desks
An insignificant person at a large wedding
Old Spice gold spitfire, spin dry lettuce or kittens

You're no slogan, you're far from an empire at peace
A valentine bullet, diploid pleadings, cretaceous
Icing teeth, smeared black ink, eyeliner, font smudged
Automatic love letters smeared on veins
My face was hacked
is so dry, can't be felt, is so red
Your demon accusers, your fear's font, mango pockets
You're like the AT&T people, or Santa Clause on Prozac
Sometimes, you're like an invisible phenomenon
Press my "like" button
You're something the lord made to sound like water
Some prefer nettles and preach Christ out of envy
Pre-cooked shrimp, chemical emeralds
Your computer guy is low on memory
Your cog disguise, cog suit, arpeggiator
resilience gem, intangible assets
I'm on a boat coming home
I'm made of wax, Larry. What are you made of?
Marigolds burrow in oil

This poem was written after Lynn Behrendt's poem " I'm Nothing and Can Therefore Never be Locked Up or Even Captured Really" as it was suggested by Google.

When did Apollonius study conic sections?
Apartment therapy
Who was the god of white nights vodka?
Hyacinthus withstands play-it-again sports
A fire escape to other planets, your balcony, your patio, your porch
The meaning of dimes and disco sticks and discretion
On your dead shores the sand is warm
How do you change his background?
Your dad was a hipster and your dog was worth it too
The demise of decision, desperate light switches
Study Island, study the word to show yourself approved
The aorta exits from which chamber of the heart again?
An example branched into the pulmonary circuit
Ultrasound uncoiled, an index of appalling strangeness
Mercy, mistranslation, an impossible ghost protocol
Cannibals in charity locations die of hate
Who unfollowed me?
Who was eliminated? Got kicked off? Voted in? Got cancer?
Who came up with the word Cubism?
Whispers gathered behind me like the color blue
Enchant, clutch, skirt
A hemlock dress washed up on the beach of a tumid river
Dimly seen trees speak to the ocean and receive silence
Magazines blown across a light orange beach
Islands dream of glaciers shaped like the world
Galapagos, Pitcairn, Faroe
The 1913 Armory Show, and the most annoying orange
Is the ankh the origin of electromagnetism?
Her ankles bones are good examples of kissing, enthesopathy
Each bird sings another grammar
Name some band names from Greek mythology
from the museum of last night

The texture of Gregorian chant suggests that meanings are determined by
wavelength, orbitals, websockets
Functional medicine, sugar pulling and sugar blowing, theatrical combat
Am I a text bunny?
An eggplant study tool in names, islands, goddesses
In the mosquito tabernacle, a bloodmoon cloak
Baby names battle bacteria and
pink robots changed the history of New York
Gratuitous space battles the nomads
Dog nose color, economy candy, French rule in Indochina
Thrift shop terriers, tiny flowers pray, silver patterns like fireflies
Dream of frost, a fat radish, frogs and peaches
How to save a fraying life
Frail heartbeats and pianos addicted to duration
Collapsed and bedazzled, jars of clay sublime
Her dresses fly too close to the ground, fall sometimes
A makeup artist makes death looks like roses
Dirty faces stream, scary kids scaring kids

Constellations, compass test, the composition of matter
The composition of one or two isometries
Superman was fabricated out of an invalid pattern completely bare
Chalksilk, Kandinsky, the blue fruit guys
Crows are hollow with theater
Fractured, death is not a parenthesis, a stopwatch
The uncanny civilization, a fragment of an analysis
Remove all doubt from these really bad eggs
Solipsism, frictional unemployment, frizzy hair
To find the percentage of an element in a compound, practice forgiveness
A basket of strawberries is oppressed by solvents
Water must reach out to become a machine of hail and sleep
Put a dictionary in the freezer
Life's clustering regressions
Balanced, unbalanced, ragged
Do shadows wear shoes? When darkness is slick, precipitous
A snow motto-ed poem with brown eyes
Study matrimonial advertisements and their lack of reluctance
Molecules that absorb light are called mothers

Hell followed the little girl into her happinesses
and how hope begs for disappointment
Whispers adhered to her and also reeked of indifference
I was carried away Pocahaunted by the human centipede
How to tie a tie and lose weight in America
Spelling adheres to the handsomest drowned man
Foamy the Squirrel runs through the hand fan museum
Stars that harden on impact, widows riddled with days

Oscillatoria overthruster dies with sleep
Each day on an average moon:
rubies, bullets, histoire des arts
In the how-to hospital, his unilateral neglect
Cloud scapula under this writing, a bed intruded by bedevilments
The best thing I ever ate? Pronunciation
Broom exponents, compare injuries
The moss won't start, lawn mow the truth
The tip of my tongue hurts. My nose is swollen
Umbrella, Australia, an iceberg owl city
Tulip junkie, onion root, atomic force microscopy
Airfoil, antler, purevolume eras
Empathetic helpful benevolent nature
An aerophone is an instrument that causes what to vibrate?
Recycling, not spraying, this puncture device
Can prophets make mistakes?
Toothpaste Trojan, the meaning in migraines
a punishing happiness, a fiver game
Particulars, healing masks, an abuse of the new moon
Cat daddy, the decapitated chicken analysis
Larry Leadfoot, Daniel Pearl, John the Baptist, Holofernes
MidgetWOW in scarlet, postsynaptic grief, inhibited reactive attachment disorder
The constant key of bone marrow
The bitter tea of General Yen
The bite sized book of bible trivia
The pink parts of Saturn's moons are the color of rhubarb
Rhyme therapy, sandman, snowman, stars, roses
A satyr hemp tycoon in primrose tweed

October leaves cover everything in a frequent and shimmering caffeine
Sunglasses in the shape of the pyramids
A font bathed in doubt, a man hanged himself on a French easel
She blushes like a blueprint
His blindness is a map of the world
His palms are sweaty with sturgeon facts
She poses in her sarcoma study dress
Islamorada, the Moonpie Sonata
Who is the goddess of science? What exactly is a normal heart?
The newspaper constellation: crimes that involve both desire and vending
Mumbai lights remake rage to look like escapism
Everything seems borrowed and empty in field flannels
Dumbbell dehiscence
Delicious heights of nox copper and the ravenettes

You are both so neutral and so soluble
Rain is when the earth is television
What percent of which pronoun do you wear?
What I really meant to say was: what does my name mean?
Evacuate all the Legos
You are thermally stable, folded up into a drinking game

This poem was written after the poem "Study" by Lynn Behrendt as it was suggested by Google.

The end of citation, swim in air tonight, in heated butterflied swing
Sinking into your tea of tears, into hasty paperbacks
I saw you tearing a paper towel from the roll
Tiger tears describe Bach's grief
What is the mood of your mouth? Picoseconds, microseconds
The killing bachelor, the mentalist mechanic, the mermaid of Venice
He's a metacritic, a metro bunny jackass
Nuns wade, a habit of nunslaughter
Bald orchids, the Middle Ages, rosary robbed, human ash
Sorghum, sortilegio, say out loud each sediment by name
How sun tolerant are your hostas, anyway? Your flowers, your ferns?
How many lipsticks will measure the distance between the sun and the earth?
Washing up on her mind's common beach:
suspensory ligaments, horseshoe crabs, horseradish
He sleeps in wire shade, a theory of a deadman
Circle proofs in latex for free
Prove to me your triangles are similar
Crooked vultures and their thangs
He is a theme park accident
Enthralled, the virgin and child sculpture where god reigns
A Madonna in isolation, her heart full of wind
A heron is eating her goldfish
A heron landing team event
Nest wine, non-verbal cues, the No Neck Blues Band
Netherwing tabard, presence, eggs
Sheenisms in maroon, a reunion in terror, condensed matter

Ostrich
Ostringstream
Ostracism
Ostrich feathers
Ostream
Ostrich fern
Ostrich meat
Ostrich facts
Ostracization

Mushroom farm, barrel harness
He's a Kaddish dove smoking rum-cured cigars, a melancholia door to three other rooms
A snowmobile has the initial velocity of what exactly?
A snot splatter guide for Neopets
Where exactly is snot stored?
Let's go storm bowling
A castle rests in its curtains
Is a natural disaster also a noun?
She neglected his nightmares, noiseless and patient
Phases and fabrics in manifest summary
What is the synonym that outshone the sun?
In her beaver beef heels, an ether bunny, medicine in yellow and black
Ghost celebrities come in threes
Crush the sky into three rooms, there are plants arranged in three rows
Is an octopus a vegetable? Is an aster a perennial?
An asteroid the size of an aspirin crashed and burned nothing
Two elliptical galaxies estimate themselves
Catalog the stars in 1924
Astrodentistry, astral projection, computational turbulent flows
He is a marathon of numbers
Dogs with bees in their mouths, fractions of train yards
Foam blushings, crime ornaments night
Oceansize the last wrongs as remnants of a church
The pelvic and leg bones of a snake
Who is god's puppeteer? An Auschwitz lullaby?
Flea goddess, true Mandalorian SmartyPigs
Two-minded clothing lost under a shattered sun
Walk through the heaven vines on the Jersey Shore
Smarter than meaning, her hair needs his Japans
His thoughts are not our thoughts, they march on
His trucks, her dolls, the shape of history
Stern diamonds warn
Is part of the what? Is also known as?
Erase discography in marble walls white as milk
She is a maroon severe macaw
Barsac is the color of foie gras, an antique numbered appellation
In magnesium magnetic moments
smile for the haters, and smack it like a Honda

Her highness, spyness, fatness in roseate ringtones
Artic skimmer, frost broken bells
The voodoo rhythms of psychobilly and sick things
He is a noun project foreshadowed with invalidism
Claes Oldenberg has a poem in his shoes
On her majesty's secret service snow globes
Her individualism was atomized into an aluminum colored dust

This poem written after my poem "In Tearooms, in the Metro" – as it was suggested by Google.

ATOMICA CROSSES THE WATER WITH
A MORPHEUS ACTION FIGURE

The butcher says, "It's anime snacktime!"
Ghostman, frost, monkeywrestle Montreal
Hunt for mushrooms in a morphine galaxy that looks like New Jersey
False freezing, then fried in butter
A flock of dimes, a mansard roof vampire weekend
Her mansion is taller than mine
A widow's walk, her tears diverted on multiple slopes
when multiplying exponents on Instapaper
Medicine got it wrong about when memory dies
Melted chocolate makes you thinner
When melody is ripe and in season
Dolphin infused vodka, insect into select
Insert pearls into an oracle, and then turn a lemon into a battery
A mason is about to expose all his secrets
Tajikistan stupidly, a mirror for Perseus, a catalyst
Almost B, barely C
His holiness's petroleum is limited
Molarity, bankrupted commas
A panicked atheism in salmon damask
The heart's curriculum
Mandarin oranges, my prophet chunders
She wears her depression mascara and
watches Madagascar penguins in a Christmas caper
Wax butterflies with the cutest personalities
Hungrynowhere, under a wrecking ball moon
The rage written in the from and to on an envelope
Igloos sewn with human summary
An example of a nonelectrolyte event
An elm and three sisters, pollen mixed with transit
The disease in this phrase, sleep strapped to his friendly attachments
Philadelphia's sunny disintegration
An alarm clock that actually cooks bacon

Hexidecimal Hawaiian Hinduism
He is comprised of a repeating self, his best sarcastic gospel
Saran wrap weight loss for Wufniks
Abandon the heart as if it were a florist
Salt means help or luck
A mouth full of gold, many of his attributes are not valid
A memory of light, or a chest to pin a medal on

Damn you, autocorrect
Damsel lace, ladder rungs
A dictionary burial at sea
Swallow death in a sentence, its ice green lava
Program logic rattles and gnarls
A man-eating and stock-picking robot
A parade of oyster and theories
I should be in French, where the days are divided by a darkroom discretion
He was finally alone with his digital dream materials, his dudeness, his divine shadow
Random number generator, ransom note generator
Android tourists sleep
Her headache was high in fat
Biblebirds, a relative's DNA like an omen machine
Plum oil, a jam colored shawl when the sun turns blue
Bacon oracle bioavailability, kiss midnight from mouth to ear
Tanning luminosity in Pythagoreanism

George Bataille, sonically speaking, said
"Arsonists get all the girls"
Say a novena to make darkness fall, to kiss girls
Hybridize that sonata. Note that her realm is closed but can be visited
Use this poem to generate random events like
throwing up, falling asleep, losing weight
Stop breathing, you are a fortune cookie cliché

This poem was written after my poem "Lady Catfish" as it was suggested by Google.

STUPID LOVE COUPON MONKEY GAMES

Nail lacquer, not just coffee, nobody wonder girls
Pigman Pharmaceuticals, pinkblack, pinballs
Black dice slip like champagne or carnations
Pinterest, eye symptoms, cake box
Whole New Mind: a princess boutique in calming colors
A chance to miss your cracks of sunlight
Or a carpenter is building a rectangular room
Or a Carpathian nightmare poem
Carpenter bees, even a sentence can be an invasive species
Speak to me in bathtub Latin
It's chilly in the Kelvin Hotel
Slush Fahrenheit, zip Cochise Appaloosa
Days fade into his hearing aids
Vocaloid shimmer, an instinct toward language leaf shower, a leather bed
or an absence of grass
It's a pronunciation polka
Invert property shark, vernacular dissent
on the conjunctivitis express
Her skin was paved in gold and indifference
Chocolate, cobblestone, cement
In corn, the trait for tall
A November filled with holes, a novena to sit still
Documentary on Nerval's apocryphal lobster
Smells like a nervous magician to me
An arranged marriage of hypertrophic scars
Make a drink out of this imperfect world: an ice merchant's dream
Never poke your uncle with a fork
Never polka with a porcupine
Polka dot cadaver, prank an anarchist
An archive of feelings, Japan at dawn
Antler velvet, this hot tub full of sheet music must be destroyed
Keep your hands to yourself – knitting is half the battle

Played his digeridoo in an illuminated Singapore
and possibly I like the thrill of pony shows
What do you do when you are bored at a royal wedding?
What is the volume of a cylinder? The value of my car?
What did we invent? What did we wear? What did we eat?
Lack of sleep, empathy, color, vitamin D, thereof
Inkheart, ink my whole body
She nicknames her pancakes and then eats them
Disappointment is free of invisible prepositions
When is the Snowager asleep in her jelly world? Her soup kitchen hole?
What causes neon tetra disease?
Pine embryo, her veins' poppy dresses
Mapping the thorax, an empress in golden woodlands, her printed palace
Czar pimp, his mouth stuffed with pronouns and promise
She is a portrait of devices
Her anxiety Yeats at my grammar
Radio heart with a roof that doesn't leak
Junk milk, she's got a sunburn for living
Sorrow formed a river, she wore YouTube around her neck
She scissors and swans in simplest forms
A period of consequences and organizing
Shell broken, pain plus dogs, logic gate
An opaque object like a war or a heart
An opal hearted country like a shell, shale wound
Moonesque, Pisces, pillow, pill addict
She calculates her love of shoes with regret trimmings
With a pocket full of shells, a pinch of salt and a
pistol in his hands
With a permit you can drive and a pair of steel toed boots
A perfectly balanced roulette wheel and a pearl earring
Pentatonic world voices like moths
A pen warmed up in hell, a pen in the dryer
that erases writing, which writes in space, which removes scratches from cars
The inkwhite where lambs are born
When the novocaine wears off and Nova Scotia lobster season is over
a plastic ark for sale
Mothballs, lemmings, juicy fruit gum
Buffalo hump black mark back bow

With a bottle of Jack before I brush my teeth
An apparent intention in the fate of an individual
Voidchorus, clowns that caper in sawdust rings
at the Clovis three dollar theatre
A horse rustled my jimmies
Rabbit dynamite rhymes. That rug tied the room together
In heaven, no skin, no shoes and her voice is no longer full of money
Her velvet vase, her very eyes, glitter in her veins
Red dust all showing

This poem was written after my poem "Craze, Novel, Pink" as it was suggested by Google.

Dashmask, sickraven, the caterpillar's soft steps
I love thee like a home burial poem
Can you really summarize the rain?
How Annandale went out and learned to sweep the floor
Haiku hunter, how to be alone with your grammar
He wants to liberate the earth from civilization
Shark tank parishioners linger in New Zealand with folded hands
Killing flies like you, the candles throw in their music
Light travels like an unwelcome discography
Fat thistles, wild with romantic swag in a republic of suffering
The end of days is a structure we can measure
Like body fat, matter, what we've lost, temperature, acres, audience
Acquainted, abbreviated, bees walk through Galileo's yellow bible
This is not meant to be a theory or a factual statement
She is miserable and microwave safe and miracle-ized
The Jesus Bible Tankini
Were we created by extraterrestrials?
Were we meant to eat meat together in a past life?
Were we just wasting broken-hearted time?
Neolithic revolution, we vote on a hypothesis of tomorrow
Hopping arctic compass parabola, Batman
Indigo, cosine, derivative, crimp, shine
Thistleheads and wrecks, even god is deprived of place
Things invented by accident:
space, the number 3, Central Park, the sky, the ocean,
this coming weekend in Manhattan
I miss the things hidden in money
Burning plasma, burning mouth syndrome
The Buddha bass tab on shiny toy guns
Lyrics yell for weed control, ignorant devices
We are not eaten by yaks, not amused and not alone

We are not statistically significant
Sticky rice lip gloss, stilettos, stillborn, stinkbugs
Starless, this is the place for the writer to handwrite their name
The river begins like a book, its scaffolding, staging
Watermark, wishwound
Two dots scream at each other
The door smiles at her amnesia bones
The wind contains additional commands, willows
Smooth orange synonyms are your horses
Outrageous drinking games involving otters
Limitless walkthrough zombie Sasquatch annihilation
Cut breath fantasy gamer
Hope is inorganic, so simple, our idleness
Is it really unlawful to duplicate this key?
An unknown mortal orchestra
Armies of artists and their alphabets
All the question marks started to sing
The Styrofoam began to melt away, and saints said "whoa"
furled this last syllable of recorded time
and the least penetrating form of radiation you should know about in English
Verses like dangerous branches
At the mall there was a séance to find the least random number
Newspapers were once ships, commonplacing
Taproots among beauties, Nike married a striping machine
Self-immolation as a photographic protest
Brightness brushes coastal bedrooms, the sky burns after reading
Shell scripts in darkness strategy
Is the light from a lightbulb coherent? The sky is polarized
Incandescent, monochromatic, ohmic
We live in an invented America
The diaper bag is also on fire
Insolence pixelated, water cycle, the weekend never dies streaming
The rose fought between the warmth of other suns
Unsaid, brides forget in slow motion
Bridesmaids carry Carnival Cruises to America
Buffoonery oxidizes
The appearance of an organism is its consensus

Guests trade silence in the facial flex dictionary
She's a sentimentality virgin in her landlocked hours
Language lives on moats, the wild Venezuela office message
Out of sleeping pills, we're deductible

This poem was written after "The Poem" by George Oppen as it was suggested by Google.

or a clothing summary of the king
Dandy acres untours pronunciation
Bracketology, a bracelet made from her teeth

Frame   moment   f r a m e

Damnation's prayer for a higher tax bill
Contagion and aftershock in a few paintballs more
Envy's minor reflection, brother velvet
A bright new room called Boise
Jerseylicious or write an autistic haiku
Her artwork is an argument with corporate poetry
What is the verb form of architect?
What is the evolved form of Archen?
What is the body form of archaebacteria?
Archimedes schnapps, wolf spiders, grannies
Synonyms rabidly devote themselves to meaning
She is pro-life curious
The barometric pressure falls
The beating heart boils and becomes greater in size
Islam blinks its eyes, burns fat, builds muscle
A spiral galaxy or a rock hen
It's a season of mutations
a characteristic
of most nonmetallic solids
of a charmed wife
of a DNA molecule
of a fixed asset
A charred glyph and no answers

Autopsy cladding hoax
An arts council as a pet?
Is a lovebird a parrot?
Postcolonial reason through a monstrous lens
A glory starfield, bewilderment, bone marrow
Bees, bitterness, a blasphemy so heartfelt that its wings broke
Bipolar with big sharp pointy teeth, she takes bites out of shade
She sleeps in birch bark sheets
A radiant tea house tunnel syndrome
Bigshot, bassbone, breathing mode, bristle disc
How do radial engines work?
Brain tumor styles, a stream braided like a prom
Thistle bear captured wow
Thoughtbot makes a fable with amber eyes
Mythology mosaics the moon
He's a cult monster rancher
Make my cake
When children look like the elderly, or cupcakes
Cloudruins, out of it, the sun like a tattoo, on the side of the road
A snack bar where the snozberries taste like snozberries
His hypothesis roars with ecology
Bleached characters smeared with kingdoms
Double vision action photography
A chair is still a chair, a chair is not a chair, a chair is just a chair
Boulevards made of paper, a nightmare facsimile
She even Nair-ed the couch legs
A yellow grammar in a year which is correct
Yarn garden, a fabric of topsoil
A yard above the knee, flexbirds
Love Teflon, laugh rift, a bare-knuckled bucket of does
Mineral necessities pinch me
Fatima of the Camillas
Swing a painting toward stable matchings
A dead magazine plastic machine
Italian balloons imagine a sky
A chair in German is still a chair, or a word
Air in the shape of a hand, or a high heel on the Scotch Tape Plains

Look at a junkyard, look for light fields
Look for her in the daytime with a flashlight
Her life improved dramatically in your hands, dude
Cardamom sober, a baby name tin teardrop coordinating conjunction
The diameter of a chord by Chopin
Liquor lab names, she throws up themed gifts
Chemistry of a cat's meow, she has a crush on an electron
The color of an opaque object in a recreational light
The warning star is an indication of the mineral powder in a polar bear's fur
The heart is a blue warning sign
the color of a construction zone, a cheetah, a license plate from Texas
A camel's tongue, a cat's gums, a calla lily, a cardinal
Amniotic aura diamonds steer heads
A mirror mineral giraffe
Crescendo cellular flowerless plants, a catapult for charades
An example of animal folklore, a seed, a pond is a cholangiogram
Dial our listen library yourself, our riotous defects on the altar of the cold war
Vergemoon, the transmigration of her tequila socks
She heard my voice in French and thought "I could be anyone"
Is that Charles Bronson on the phone?
Reverse lookup her charms, her Chardonnays
Oxalic acid, orangette, silverbeet
Take out, carrier pigeon, carrot cream oil
Scalextric acidlullabye
High performance butterfly valves
Anodize really bad eggs into achievement
Right now everything you want is wrong
Her gossip parts throatlatched, a rally to nowhere
Killing swans by an asphalt assembly
A continuous integration of thematic units
Which light is least effective in photosynthesis?
The color left behind depends on what? Nonattainment areas
Your life imitates a guitar, a notational velocity
Ragas, chess games, Gregorian chants
With its hat about its ears, and an emphasis on the super fan
Invert grammar, an apostrophe addiction

Unblock the winter, and her semi-charmed laying machine
A thank you note that you may believe was written in a meadow of crabs
Remove dead traces of scribblenauts
then splatter, giggle

This poem was written after my poem "Julian's Idyll" as it was suggested by Google.

HER HAIR WAS THE COLOR
OF A CHARCOAL FILTER

She replaces the pool water with pee
We are in the theater of chance now
Hope embraced her mistakes
She thinks she has control over all shapes of water
She takes the trees for granted, has crushes with Croatian subtitles
America has been bamboozled by a nectar of baseball references
America rehearses
She made a temple out of tires for the Cat Goddess
Her red pyramids name the wind like a radio
Rehab is a rehypothesis, dinnerdress her a little
Spell "rehypothocation" on an empty stage, without an audience
Sableye, antelope goggles, helicopter, herbicide
Sliced bread and strangling isn't an option
Stop smoking, start drinking, since steroid hormones are lipids
This sentence loves you
Start a sentence with "a ballroom startles easily" and go from there
The idea of heaven could easily be a disease reflex
Her anxiety is an acoustic apparatus
A witch, a dog, a baby, a cat, a goat, a horse
Startle it

Peat, willows, eels
Make up some statistics about them on the spot
If you look up tonight, the stars wear no makeup
Black holes organize into a pattern
Satellites event and twinkle
Snowflakes fell in perfect stripes
Scorpion star clusters fell like sand, laid out like starfish
Start a sentence with "a religion of doors"
Windows normally do nothing, windows are not like a parade
Goodbyes stuck into her skin, her life cycle began with indifference

Nautical twilight, small wars smuggled like smart chargers
She was afflicted by meaning
And boom goes the dynamite family guy in the marriage hearse
Bliss blizzard, blink tiger, melon light, pig barber
Electrical significance, shock stretches her character
There is friction in her addresses
a kinetic analysis
Even after 65 days in a sugarcult, his rhymes are not appealing
Fevers, rashes, thumb deformities
Four lights on and no children
There are worse things I could have purchased on my iPhone
There are two kinds of people, three parties to a check, and several isotopes
Trees mistaken for transitional fossils
There are trap doors among us
Are teeth also a fruit?
Are tanning beds poisonous?
Are trampolines tax deductible?
Are travel agents really worth it?
Cultivate wheat, puppeteer death clips, there is evidence of love in the urine
Biblefire, virulent bacteriophage
She's a limelight kisser
What are the lyrics to these fireworks?
Pressure gradient, sliverswell, cyclone amusement
Laughter assaults American grains
A desert asymmetry, an astronaut farmer
An astronomical unit is really an asteroid belt
Astigmatism and the astrology of beer
What is your compatibility to day?
The invention of pronunciation, a sonata in D minor
There are plenty of fish
Who played Hitler in a high school musical?
Clancyness, his cereal never gets soggy
Ribbon fractures, inflatable boats, injuries from coughing
Instead happily explore the attractive toys
She was a heavy cream bride
Her Helvetica heart, coral-boned
Headless mice sing in handcuffs

Her immunity was invisible, her income elastic
A weather halo interpolated light
No sebaceous threshold, pigmented, navigated, narrative
Tramadol thrust, ghost crush, collapse
Horses in calm review, three months of Thai horror
The stars are projectors, dustmoon, inerrancy
On inertial motion on a rotating sphere
Silver breaks easily, electric easy tea, our entangling breath
Oil droplets oscillate, circadian rhythms, chatclash
Bring your own bright star

This poem was written after my poem "Can-Am Series" as it was suggested by Google.

Moss enchanted these language tombs
Gods wear jewelry on their museum visits
What were their origins?
What was their outlook on the afterlife?
Oracle ointment, Pentacost, Orientalizing periods
How many calories are in New York?
The tongue offers sugar money, a sienna-ed sun
Indifference burned and smelled like antifreeze
Angulate tortoises, blistered lips
Peace bruised sin in the dictionary
This shocking story, shattered and soggy with virgin swimmings
And since you can't escape me, do I ever cross your mind?
And since I am dead I can take off my head
My name in math, in Nougatine
Nouvelle vague, a bias generator
Birds mimic the sympathetic nervous system
Matter is classified as a pair of boots
Her fact practice, shards of vinyl spirits donate their bones
The day passed like a chapter summary
Only one state has no McDonalds
Only one state has no national park
Time became stale with stunts
There are online stuttering activities in maroon
Morale-grey, cyber-November is the color of noodles
Nightingales weep on the consequence of meaning
How do I capitalize the moon?
How can I keep from singing? Or slapping?
How can I be taller? Or make more money?
How clean is my house? How could my hair grow faster?
Could my saucepans bring on menopause?
Black sunburned purple yellow

Closed, washed out, blurry, watering, beyond seeing, bleeding
Are your eyes too small for contacts? Can your eyes be transplanted to a friend?
Pawn stars, recruited and funky, be my escape

Facebook is tickfree

When bored or reading, dieting, ovulating, raining, running
the weather is thirsty for Adderall
When they are caught, they are thrown away
Our jobs reminisce over us
These lines should be caged at night
Flying DramaWiki noble masters made of meat
Eggmen tucked into cannons
Zombie imitators are also sons of god
Charming gardeners of the underworld
Are thongs comfortable? Are the seasons capitalized?
Are the Poughkeepsie Tapes real? Are the Knicks in the playoffs?
Are the colon and the large intestine the same thing?
Coyotes are moving to Winnipeg

Starfish
Stars from hottest to coolest
Star Trek uniforms
Starling eggs
Stains

Starless and sunless ballrooms, and their failed light

Smoothing methods, statistical manifold, sampling theorem
This is a notational form of decay
He subtracts from her surface brightness
Optic citation, meridian, her belly her skin
On Monday or in Monday grammar
Throw best price thresher shark
The miles are threadless, thrillist
Let's throw knives and throw pillows at her cancer
Struggle tabs, her blood was silver
Sloe slip rings, sliding doors, slant drilling
Dressed in slats, strangle wisteria

What materials are you fingernails made of?
Widows weaving wreathes, wattle whistle, wide brimmed
She said, "Money is like us"
Mooncake phases, a sonata, a palace filled with chattel
Swoon, sow, sorrow
Two slowniks sewn together – what is their moon sign compatibility?
Snow White, her salted lovesickness, wings and roots
curates Tanya's disastrous taste in electrical circuits
A taxidermied alchemist teaching lessons in Go
Bourbon under the stars
A halophile is responsible for these spoiling juices
Egyptian agriculture, washing pictures, Moses wasps

A traveler's anthology
A god
A history
A novel
A river

Turner painted the water in our bodies as
porcelain and graphite castles
There is an ossification in Bone Lick Park
An ivory orchard full of oracles, possibly tucked in
Wig Runescape, cracked wasabi, glass powder
The rain on your skin and you do it anyway
This song is sick and this is why you are fat
It might be that I'm holding your hand but holding it a little too loose
Fossils and towels, the smell of shade
A town called Alice or Panic
A cocktail of sand, brainticket black, pineal gland
Lightheaded, sequential type unconnected, sensebowl
SurroundSushi, superfood suppression
Both atomic bombs, 4 years on an island, his wife, a tornado, rabies
Neverland necrotizes, an unmediated decay
The 10 commandments or 10 things I hate about you or 10 ragas to a disco beat
10 raw eggs, 10 raw potatoes with a longjaw mud snapper
Linseed oil and lemon bars and lettuce wraps
There are some letters spacing out in a word
There is a whitehot heart whispered in every story

Name when all the continents were together
Name when you die
Name when I arrive
Name when a bowl is not microwave safe
A billion Chinese jump and one body part is injured
Lemons, white rice, pebbles and moss, cherries, onions
Her arms amputated around me
Heavy weak numb tired tingly on fire, like home
They are asleep, they are burning,
Something is stuck in my throat, in my eye
Somebody is stuck in my chest, is crawling on my skin, is staring at me, is biting me
The structure of falling asleep, in my rearview seas

This poem was written after my poem "Ella Etruscan Olives Burnt and Sien(n)a" as it was suggested by Google.

Salmonella compass points to "Her Thighs: The Movie"
Two Karmapas clean a farm house
And then the weather turns into a karma loop
Yoga police pull her over on the Havanese Highway near the Houdini Hair Salon
Hookah Lounge, herbal sandal turmeric, hopstop
She wears a necklace in the shape of a medical event
She wants to buy Hello Kitty Health Insurance™ at the Hotel Concorde Saint Lazare
Her diamond and fearful symmetry
Her car won't start, her calf, her cancer
Her cardboard lover tampered and stalled
Calpahlon corporation laceration recall
Cheek activator unloader, pickup summer-proof eyeliner
The Philippines are transparent with cakes and pants and salaries
She is a collagist of miracle movie deaths
We are stuck on Monologue Mountain where she buys Tragic Marionette sheet music
Goldworks, games crush her castles
She keeps an ever-growing archive of god in her garage
Allwheel protectant giveaway
One basketball was in Latin and her other shoe was all made of logic
Grammar is just a set of probabilities
She both grows fruit and doesn't bloom
Grout a Norwegian, the girl vs. snake compatibility
Adhesive mixed with an awesome god in an abominable church
A goat, also the trees could have been lyrics
and yet we are alive in Egypt doing Elvis Presley
Her arrows of outrageous fortune point down
Lunar laundry starch lemon meringue
Let me watch this
Let's change clothes, chase each other around the room, change the world
Her vampire husband sounds like a voice full of money, a Van Cleef indicator
Nasturtiums and clematis climb in contraction, in her intestines
Charm City, Charmglow
Butterfly purple enamel "But I'm a cheerleader" injections

The nuns are watching, then I got high
The cat came back as a fruit spirit
The midwives feared god
Harmonic sequences in the Math Hamster Motel
His hand-painted Christmas balls, his roughleaf dogwood
These three miles were treated the same size as earth
Florescent walls
The Torah girls were giants after the flood
Giant hogweed girlsense with a madness for dimes
Incentives toward acrostic, surgical bras, compression garments
Her tag is sticking out
Her trombone, her trumpet, her town too
Married less than one year divorce
Married less than six months taxes
Let's all chant and go down to the river
Let's advertise this hell
Add a garter border
Two men and a truck, two peas in a bucket, two cups of sleep
James Joyce at the gates of sleep
Garnishments swim side by side
If she wears two garter belts, which one do I throw?
Ouija-sama
What gear to I need to hunt feral pigs?
To help with shin splints?
Her art nested with amputations
Her arms were missing from birth
Feathering nicotine levels, galaxy gramophones
A crooked sky, a botanical slimming gel
Both right handed and left handed Rancido's Deep Journey dub
Cards games murmur, heat mocked
Meteorologist Gets Last Laugh, chicken legs and their meaning
The death of time, the idea of pre-paid medical
The Ah Bra AsSeenOnTV as a form of lucid dreaming
The ash in ligature, an informal pattern
Use these Chinese batteries in a sentence
Her hair was hazard colored, a vagrant superstition
Her soul was swollen with karaoke

Her chariot was an empty hazelnut
Oak barrels pineapple rib Timonium
Tackle warehouse, tacky Christmas sweaters
Definitions quilted with meaning, a stainless Austria
on ice, without makeup
Two lions napped on the porch and buried her like a failure
Harnesshames and harmonics to cypress echo

This poem was written after my poem "Graham Cracker Ragas" as it was suggested by Bing.

A COLLAGIST TAGGED THE SKY

The sagas break like a new moon covered in tickets
Hammer camp WoW, auto parts and her ankle rehab
True stick death, slow seasons, sunswim lyric
A slender man in the slipper room near a slanted door
Heartgold, Mister Seed's Good Deals
Tin pant liquidator, trauma model, wig twins
Twirls and twigs, Twirl Mania, twirl a squirrel
When was Jesus really born?
When was the internet invented?
Was it before cakes, figurines, and painted furniture?
Couture diddles spice, bras stamped with pets
The thesaurus dies with our thirst mechanism
Mozart mutts, ghostly other people do the killing
Impossible bad things in French and you were someone else
A moth sailboat that looks like a bee in your ear
A hummingbird problem in my closet
Her Sundays were outfitted with prednisone
She invented a myth to explain that gym in Las Vegas
An infestation of orchids and pictures
Identification traps, bridal dresses cut into years
Your ticket has been escalated, a diet without a permit
Herpes bags, a constructivist method of parenting
My twitching eye married the blue sky
Dogs eat grass in Whyville
Why is wisdom personified as a woman in Illinois jokes?
Why won't her teeth bloom?
Why does the washing machine get out of balance?
Why wash meat?
Why wash off the mosquito repellant?
Wishbones are charms, in monochrome 10 bridges burn
Wishmaster envelopes willed with prayers
Mint and rue, Swansboro garment songs
Wood mushrooms hymn under wings to an incense that smells like jeans

The compassion in sewing tape
Of the Month clubs for Siberians
Miracle Tiber on the corner of Bitter and Sweet
Little shadows, lithotripsy, hollowing tools: the ultimate rarities in her heart
My life is stupid, sexist, horrible, terrible, like soccer
Is shyness a sin or a sign of love?
The shyness in Japanese bedrooms, small packages in smoky places
Smackdown dental with green stars smocking
The snow is falling
Love cake topper, blue blazer style, gifts, blessings, boyfriends
Crocodile sayings, black curtains, pure imagination
Andromeda written on a chart of measures
Horse games for girls
and then Tango made three
The valley shook and none walked through
There were fewer bands, the Mysterians' greater use for love was like a lotion
The outside of the house was covered in moonflowers, moth wings
They lived one day like it was orange
Softshelled under a billboard moon
Magic scoop best price

An unfinished husband, you are an oasis in collapse
Islands strung like chapter summaries, an idle stroll
Sometimes her flesh lived in the fun lane

A god
A check
A man
A grant
A Chevrolet

The forbidden fortunes in Western wear

You have been closed
You were selected but not displayed
You became the formalist portal of god
You contained validation errors

You were a French overture or a city
You were mostly usable to plants
You were a business letter, a sonnet, a large glass window
You were a series of anatomy or haiku
You were witchcraft or an affidavit
You were godliness, ownership, government
You were an address, also autism and art
You were an exact equation of anemia in Mediterranean women
Elegy, ellipse, essay
Your eyes were layered in old anesthetic, in ecological sequences
Your membranes were empathetic, benevolent and helpful
Your elegant dentistry never forgot
Your biography is an ontological argument
Your shirred, your shirt says costume
What value is deanimation to a microbe?
You protect the world from destruction with unspecified powers
Your inventoried uncertainty
Open a pecan with a knife in an orange porch cartoon
You both worship and ignore dreams
Your colorized Christmases were canceled, then your white Christmas was colorized
Your whiskies were invented in churches, used as the fluid in magnetic compasses

This poem was written after my poem "Twilight's Hem" as it was suggested by Bing.

Acts, posters, costumes
Free Johnny Cash from predetermined dance steps
Dog kites do Brazil
DollieCrave fonts in doll school
School Island, scandalous folders
Field studies in a deaf font for lady machines
For you, I will party
Your legs in consideration, broadcast the self
Vindicator and restless, refuse patdown
Dress tomorrow in photos of yourself
Plus-sized pink suits slay dragons
Foot locker, meat dress, bad romance, marshmallow
Peeptoe, preparing newly woven silk, personal protection devices
Sunflower cake diorama
Show some mercy in your shooting games
Show a machine gun cartridge with a belt
Show a machine that makes marbles
Show Tokyo on a map
Show science projects with examples
Show how peeps are made
An example of solicited paper
The dogs ate crumbs from the table on the day you were born
Believe and tremble as even the dirt breathed
Wing, hull, effect
Whitening crankbaits obscura
ProblemWoW, sky beads, soft coated, wheaten cleat grass
Place dreaming in photography
Play Halloween hangman
Service codes act as the execution of hope
The articulation of skulls as dogs return to Auburn Hills, to a refuge in Hawaii
Places, occasions, papillons de nuit
When an object's velocity decreases and a bone is forced out of its joint
Throughout the body twice a year or twice a century
At the beginning or end of a sentence
The naps on the porch buried me between failures and bread

Sundays in equal shades of Johnsian greys
Between Spain and France, between spoiled meat and bleach
time's theme song sung in zebra cocktail rings
Circle gas station in Massapequa
Drinking games, volcanos, radios
Splatter spiders, mad spellers of the world untie
Mud spells, spells that work, spells to become a vampire
Potions and curses for beginners
Spells to make someone fall in love with you or become a mermaid
Spells to lose weight or get what you want
I have trouble swallowing and trouble sleeping
Breathing is a friend in free pools
Do webcams show affection?
Circus midget swallowed by hippo
Travertine showers transferred to canvas
Photos trapped by money, artists that allow trust
Auto tune changed the world with recycled materials
Artists used Adirondack colors to worship the devil and carve on gourds
Properties of sermons, idiomatic stretching exercises
Manuscripts tattooed in summary
A cave on fire with gold voices and mirrors
Microwave the entire world, or the Philippines
The farseeing inevitable Palestinian eye
then the 13th sense of fire, the price of silver in perfect Spanish
Perfect continuous preparedness
Show Surprise, AZ on a map
The surprising places where germs live with their party invitations
Tables and dreaming, her tongue along a tulip tree
Bargain with collective nouns
There are demands in these letters, paper about argon, papillons
Lanterns, snowflake shredder, skirting
Scissorboy, game show theme songs
There's a game show about bribery at a checkpoint
A game show or a poem about telling the truth, lying, god, inventions
The chenille that underlies our consciousness
The wild boars in his managerial work and his volcanism
Pillowcase dress tracing paper, a theory of pain that tessellates and pain perception
Birds fly like friendship bracelets and devil pumpkins

Pseudopods hunger for lost Christmases
There are new ways to rob you now
No flesh, no feathers, no pedigrees, no eyes
Her heart has a grammar, reached its carrying capacity, has always eaten meat
Hummingbird excretory systems
We could hear her from a hole in the earth
Box anatomy, martyr recognition software
No pictures of buttercups or powderpuffs while the nuns are watching
Spectacular pronouns and praying mantises
A problem was detected in your prayers
The tongue is the enemy of the neck, the Fatimas in birthdays
Categorical imperative, restraint seclusion
The normalization of verbshows to come, to sleep
Peephole reverser, plaster walls are her money clothing
Soar manor, magic seaweed, slot machine cherry master odds
Antenna and wing hobbies, her pronunciation was waterblocked
Red remover walkthrough, red reverence daylily
A man in a ruffled satin shirt talks to Bigfoot
Rufflebutts, her infinity skirts, Winehouse toxicology
Wind and moment frame building, blur effect
Backwater bowfishing
And I'll follow that thing in the mall wearing pearls, crying white tears
A guide to gas pumps, the history of computers
An illuminated clock against the sky, a warning found and decoded
Illuminescence causes a burning sensation
How did that squirrel get into the toilet?
Toothpick thesaurus for Cotton Eyed Joe, eggs the exact color of your bedroom color
Sun distance, moon distance
Help a monkey cross or river, or prevent a malicious code from running
Help with dust mites, car payments, yardism, snoring, dying
Suicidal thoughts, sunburn, sugar addiction, subtracting fractions
Shivering hearts with sugar on top
Sullenness, suspicion, professional eligibility
Show animal blow dryers, her alphabets abuse facts
Rump roast mistakes, tremors in hands, dogs and movies
Brothers soothe their thumbs like they had Christ's hands
I'm going on a bear hunt through my own concerns
without health insurance, without sleep, without cable

Wordgarden wildtangent, there are regrets in her shoes
Can you weld with a car battery?
Without and without medical abbreviations under an animated sun
I need an evil pet name for WoW, or evening work, or an evergreen shrub
An evening gown covers her scarred chest
Everywhere I go, Hollywood is undead, plastic surgery gone wrong in plastic patterns
special occasion diseases, speculative writing prompts
Walkthrough untrue nightmares, treasure locations, piebald pond hockey
She's a peel and stick wall border
She's tuckered out with pirate days
Muscles of the body, of the face, of the back, of the bottom of the foot
Show the muscle going to the supraspinous fossa
Static stretches underwater bowling
With water, to do at home, with magnets, with dry ice, with eggs, with light
A recycled Christ regarded as inquiry
Nylon ladder, octopus socks
Bulgarian paintball with a twist
An elastic waistband, hidden platform boots, amputee warmers
A woman that lets a dog knot her legs
Diamonds swell and feel heavy, legs that describe the whole world

Describe briefly:
Your standards for success
How blood flows through your heart
What being in love with Benjamin Franklin feels like

Scared, surprised, short of breath, smothered with a pillow
Stretched by god, stretched on the rack, stretched film wrinkling
A canvas of sciatica
Is the holy spirit in Easter baskets too?
Mother omega god, cross stitch dog pattern
Danger Mouse, Sunday punch radio portal
Telling from tin type, stone sours and their meanings
Crystals, bones, gems, meanings
Stoned at McDonald's again
Atlantic county evacuation, coloring produces too much insulin
Piercing printable secrets
Yoga exhale, inhaled corticosteroids, in apparel for dwelling

Nevada ghost towns inhibited by nitric acid
The gold can stay, truth noodles holidays
After death, philosophy and nonexistence
circa 1940 with a velvet cinema seat

The circumference of a circle
Angel wings and animal eyes
Anatomically correct bisque wire joints
Vintage anatomy patterns and another way to die
Another word for pretty, problem, perfect, party, proud, pain-positive
What's another word for perpendicular?
When your friend cheats with words and food
Today is devotional
Is there a word for people who use big words and are never wrong?
For painted tinware?
For pet loss?
The backlash started with an overhead crane and a $300 snap-on smile
Wild Alaska flying pig marathon, ants on a spaghetti monster
Unitards and leotards, chin up bars, carrots, teeterboard catcher
This amorous sweet reluctant decay, obvious strategies in a pathless woods
An undone violet, thermocouple skimmers
Pinball and pit bulls
In circus terms, what is cherry pie?
Hinge repair, the history of the unslept, ocean liners
darksiders walk through a rabbit theater
Cadaver the Clown is for sale
Record names and dates on this sugarcane field
The Hindustan Times flies with hummingbirds
Spontaneous combustion coupled with invisibility technology
Her muscles twitch toward bankruptcy
Metamaterials, eagle fables with eggs
Our light is what makes us artists and it's also what lights up a '59 Ford
There was light in a box on an August piazza
Crochet stitches and circumcision
Circus acts like Senorita Sanchez and the Bounding Rope
Parade float viewing from a petal cottage
Poets born after 1960 who committed suicide and are still alive
Fortune teller fish, paper games sayings, career paths ghost towns

Cracking whip duo lift snakes hand to hand
Woman starts fight over chicken nuggets and ends up glued to the toilet for two years
Horse meanings on a terrace overlooking a city
Pedestal costume on a mountain different country
Motivational speakers without arms or legs
Half a body, without a country, no face
Man with no ears joke
No bake cookies, no hands, no call list
There are no predictions in his eyes
Copper toxicity, crinkle wrinkle when I smile
Cigarette pants for women
Crime scenes build themselves
Eternal beads of light and refraction
Coefficient charms, circular waves on a straight mirror
Offshore coupons form an optical wind
Foldable girls, she failed to show the flamenco in her drawers
Steelhead in a prophetic anointing, skindex
A candy luminous analysis, yellow pink and blue and full of ships
This party evolved from stones

This poem was written based on Peep/Show search terms as it was suggested by Bing.

Luna legs, amour oral paroles
Honey John, the cicada Baptist
An author's purpose in using rhetoric
An audio recording device cannot be found
An Austrian went yodeling
An audience with the arcanist
An autosomal recessive disorder in five chapters
A kitchen oil fire for Hitler, a kitchen prayer
Lawn ornaments, glam cupcakes in Dubai couture
In the vacation dictionary: koa, kabob, kush
She swears like candy in her cancer cardigan
Cancellations, the taxonomy of a tall red king
Her true fitness could be vented out the chimney, her anti-sweat valves
Vortexing baffles, his chafing stick, his word for "melt"
A painting of antique gold cheese in acrylics
An animal that starts with the letter N
This antique Chinese coin will bring you wealth or a sequence in blood

An anticline trap
An anticline has beds that dip
An anticline is a fold in which

Antic Indian handmade knives
Items sin and itchy tiny spots on the bottom of her feet
Any any any gold right now above the stomach, right below the braline
He needs to figure himself out
He wants to leave his wife but doesn't
He likes her and then doesn't call
He needs a break
He is Jesus
Puppy snips, interchangeable needles, synthetic deer horns
Civilization timeline, creation myths, child mummies
Chainlove cattery, King Humbert's mottled virus

Yellow streak futurity, red spots
Can a yawn be a tic?
Yawn station Christmas tree farm
While exercising
While singing
When nervous
Invitations to farm ponds in Greek mythology
Antifacts, artist insurance in America, her chess-colored hair
Canny automatic strapping machine
Trash the Dress Boutique
Anti-waiting lounge, akinesia, be a Thin Mint Girl Scout
Chant and be happy or chant against apartheid
Addicting games, clustering clouds
Use "seedfolks" or "daily life" in a sentence
A kid in a wheelchair does a backflip
In what country is chewing gum illegal?
Cinema, winking lizard bingo, princess stealing dragons

      Kiwi the bird
      Kiwi the clown
      Kiwi the animal
      Kiwi the fruit

Carving knives in thunder boot camp
Wishweird noises sit on tiny cream sofas in front of tinted windows
Grab a bird's tail that carries messages through our bodies

This poem was written after my poem "Loco Locust" as it was suggested by Bing.

A witch and a cat pattern
Dark meat doll decoration
Stuffed with feelings, he unbuttons his pants
Guava, grapes
Taxidermy, witches' legs
Stuffed with Love Taxidermy: No Pet Too Small
Mac 'n cheese, mashed potatoes
Fat suit, rice, poblano peppers, spinach and cranberry, smoked whitefish
Dreams and beer for god, a lame of god
A lake of melanin causes skin to whiten in an invented Virginia
A lace of rage documentary, a lake of wooden tears
A lake becomes a brown black forest, a blouseblack building
contains four distinct types of fish described in great detail
Duck mind, dock lantern
The electric history of escape
Font cap, flashlight, front wig, glass chimneys
lake juice, marker lights, memory under the ocean, padlock, pilgrim
A lake running through cities, switch keys, name belt, railroad lanterns
A semaphore that is protected from receiving
Tranquility without larceny
Dogs can go to fish, drain east to west
Without water, whalers without fire, a bird reflection, someone gets hit by a car
Cupcakes filled with the holy spirit
All the fullness and goodness of a potential crises
The corresponding content of anger and amino acids
Chutzpah candy
She is an excitement hymn, with the ennui of eggs gourami
Fun, fear, fizz, crossword fascination like an aquarium
His holy spirit cartoons with happiness
The iridescence in ingenious, indignant thought
Her joy is personalized on tin buckets, on tote bags
Kodak playsport waterproof mixed feelings
She is filled with new coolant but little heat
baptized open-minded without measure

Quince jam, the rage and regret in regular gas instead of diesel
reverence, holyspirit special effects
Vegetables, goat violence, full of wonder, awestruck wonder
There is a room decorated for Princess Tinkerbell
in dark purple and yellow
in dark purple and light orange
in Hello Kitty!
A room full of brass mirrors and violets
A room has four corners, each corner has a girl
A room in summary, in abstract design
A room made of windows in Toronto
No one can enter nearby
A rook piercing, the color velvet somewhere, swept white
Reliableremodeler
A room a mile long that heals Binghamton
A roomy car for an obese person that's 178 feet long
A room filled with legos and guys and stars
Balloons, smoke, candles, money, water, books, pianos, glitter
cheese sauce, dollars, flies, ghosts, trampolines
Lion rampant azure (quarterly)
or an extended crested butte
The beautiful nightmare in a sonic toothbrush
Probability gated with words
Griffinrampant, armed and language sable
Or am I just a roadblock standing still in Calabasas?
Oyster seas, am I origami or part of the disease?
Total permanent matrixdectomy, a proper mix of employees
A quick advance in quasi-permanent, quasi-experimental design
Lyrics shattered like tickets, tour dates
As nails, as Jane, as mutually agreed, a long black magic test
Travel at the beginning of a sentence
Orca vs. blade mandolin review
Triangle woman, if you are one
Birds in the alchemist motorcycle club
Their meanings: signs, birds, frogs
Birds are bad luck coming into your house, knocking on your windows
Birds, bats, butterflies, boots
Crows classified as women's clothing

Dictionary dresses, dead spiders, define a villain's shoes
Four red feathers, a raven's feather
The graffiti in Gucci red and green sandals, K-Swiss orange and white tennis shoes
A list of luna moths over a luncheon prayer, theatre lunar elite
The bad luck of owls in war
The predictions in parakeets, in pull-on steeltoed workboots
Omens related to rabbits, in the throbbing of your right eyebrow
in rainboots, in robins hitting the window, regard cardinal feathers
Saluki syndrome, petite clothes and swarms of mosquitos
Two doves in rugged gingham black
To hear a dog whining and no dog
The abomination in film
Omens involving hawks, wallets, the world Cup soccer schedule, force limbs exploding
A summary in geisha amnesia
The universal lesson of biography and depression
Books fetter black dragonflight bedding
Collage frame, the definition of opals in dysfunctional people
Dictionary avenir, examples, essays found in a bathtub
Give attention to, intercultural, which literary device to write to
holocaust survivors
I was ink in China, an idea about black and white photography in the Himalayas
Our Shanghai correspondence written like children in the present tense
Meaning made into movies and mental illness
My father is Missouri, autobiography vs. personal narrative
Neo-angled, geisha-full text, prince consort death
The internet is also a quote bush
Remember me in a script that looks like Rhodesia
A stately toilet sings onstage, the Sherman syllabi, lullaby
Undermount
The internet is also a burning quote bush

This poem was made from my notebook of Google searches as it was suggested by Bing.

photo of the author in the Widow Jane Mine at Century House, by Franco Vogt

ANNE GORRICK is a writer and visual artist.

She is the author of several books including most recently: *The Olfactions: Poems on Perfume* (BlazeVOX Books, 2017), and *A's Visuality* (BlazeVOX, 2015). She co-edited (with Sam Truitt) *In|Filtration: An Anthology of Innovative Writing from the Hudson River Valley* (Station Hill Press, 2016).

She has collaborated with artist Cynthia Winika to produce a limited edition artists' book, *"Swans, the ice," she said,* funded by the Women's Studio Workshop in Rosendale, NY and the New York Foundation for the Arts. She has also collaborated on in-depth visual and textual projects with Scott Helmes and John Bloomberg-Rissman.

With Melanie Klein, she curates the reading series "Process to Text," which focuses on innovative writing from in and around New York's Hudson Valley.

She is a past President, and continuing member of the Board of Trustees at Century House Historical Society, home of the Widow Jane Mine, an all-volunteer organization (www.centuryhouse.org) that presents a variety of arts events (including the annual Subterranean Poetry Festival), and preserves the history of the now-defunct local cement industry.

Anne Gorrick lives in West Park, New York.

PROCESSUAL NOTE:

These poems began in 2011 with an investigation into John Cage's adventures with chance. I was working at the State University of New York at New Paltz, and we had a small museum, the Samuel Dorsky Museum of Art, with a regular exhibition called "Reading Objects." The idea of the show is to explore and expand on what is traditionally said on those little cards next to paintings. So we were presented with an array of visual work, and could pick pieces to write about. I decided to write something to accompany a musical score by Cage that was to be part of exhibition. I wrote something, and I came to hate it. This poem was displayed next to Cage's score. I felt I didn't nearly go far enough with the poem to really engage with Cage. So I started again by researching Cage, and I also spent time with Jackson Mac Low's Representative Works.

Around this time, I began to notice and find myself entertained by the way search engines attempted to anticipate our needs (it's gotten a lot better since then, and it would not be possible to find these poems now). I began to slowly type lines of poetry (eventually working my way toward entire short poems) into Google and Bing search boxes, and laugh my way through the dropdown list of wrongly anticipated results that appeared underneath my search. I began to make poems out of these search results. At first, I thought I was adding chance into the poem, but I came to realize it was just the opposite: these search results came from the zeitgeist's algorithmic desire, not my own, which ended up expanding the possibilities for the poem. The poetic "I" dissolves in this desire.

I was invited to give a reading at the museum, so I read the first poem I wrote (that I now disliked), read the new poem I made out of the old one (by pouring the first into search engines and working with the results), and invited the audience to participate in the Mac Low performance poem "Is That Wool Hat My Hat."

POETICS AND PROCESS:
A CONVERSATION WITH ANNE GORRICK
AND LYNNE DESILVA-JOHNSON

Why are you a poet?

I never really had a choice. I've been playing with language since I was a little kid. It's been one of my greatest joys, and also something that has saved my life. My parents played with it only insofar as it was a game. I've been writing since I acquired language. Poetry is the most plastic form of language for me, but my work is veering off to become more sentence-y in the past few years. We have the capacity to "mean" much more, more multi-valently than linear, utilitarian language allows, that language can hold many opposing ideas at once.

When did you decide you were a poet (and/or: do you feel comfortable calling yourself a poet, what other titles or affiliations do you prefer/feel are more accurate)?

I've been calling myself a writer or poet since forever. But am also a visual artist for the past 20+ years, working mostly in monotype printmaking using encaustic ("to burn" from the Greek) materials (beeswax, resin and pigment). I've also worked in painting, film and sound Also scent. You should smell the jasmine wax I have in my studio right now! I am ardent toward materiality, working mostly on paper. Paper contains light.

What's a "poet", anyway? What is the role of the poet today?
What do you see as your cultural and social role (in the poetry community and beyond)?

We are singers and makers by etymology. As the world gets more visual, language and sound are being left behind. In a way, being left behind is a good thing, as late-stage rapacious capitalism leaves poetry alone. It's about as contrarian as you can get right now to spend time on something that has essentially no efficient return, very little monetary transactionality. Our role is to praise and witness. To be present (which these days isn't easy). Maybe our largest role is to show the possibilities of living/writing/arting possibly.

Talk about the process or instinct to move these poems (or your work in general) as independent entities into a body of work. How and why did this happen? Have you had this intention for a while? What en- couraged and/or confounded this (or a book, in general) coming together? Was it a struggle?

These poems are like an art installation made from the garbage, junk you might find in and around a body of water (like the Hudson, which I live near). As I explained more in the process note in this book, the text is plucked from the drop-down boxes in search engines after I input lines of various text (mostly poems, but not always). The text is then edited down to the poems. If I tried to engage with the same process now with the same generative text, I'd come up with completely different poems, as the search algorithms would find the newest and latest output. The electronic zeitgeist changes constantly, like a river. I'm riveted by the temporality of this unrepeatable experiment.

About a third of the words in this book are not recognized by Word, so that seemed like a triumph around a textual canon. The first two poems include words like:

nimblewilled pineboy Smirky Brineshrimpdirect Smokesmash shantybisque Understones stiltsville Storkcraft riskmetrics vicodin Mintymix skyrim slingbox Libelula photobiographies Regretsy Whimsicle fuckery grooveshark invincibles Regalessia writhings tomatometer danglesauce

When I posted these on Facebook at one point, poet Susanna Gardner wrote: "Regretsy Whimsicle fuckery is what we all should be having."

Let me include here a direct example of how poems from *An Absence* came into its being/body. Each poem started with another poem or text (art makes more art!). In the photo below, you can see the text I began with on the left. This was poured slowly into a search engine. I used to co-curate an electronic journal called *Peep/Show,* and we had this visitor counter on it that would save all the search terms people used to find us. Based on the words "Peep/Show," I could create voluptuous lists that included circus and porn and poetry terms (you can even see a title of a Leslie Scalapino book here: THE DIHEDRONS GAZELLE-DIHEDRALS ZOOM). On the right is some of the stuff spit out of the search engine drop down box, and then I would edit it down (sometimes a lot, sometimes very little).

P/S Search Words up to 2,108
8/24/2010

Circus freak doll
School for young ladies, p/s machine
p/s sculpture
P/S the event
the dihedrons gazelle-dihedrals zoom
camera zoom peep
ocean sky soft green
"sense of place occurs then at...cture betwe
violet racked starling
zoom peep
circus ring of fie
circus curtain
m-u-d spells trouble show .com of peep
circus midway photos
/trapeze artists
/the illustrated man
poem peep in to the future
p/s surprise
peep artist under the table
sign footings
/p/s vegetable collection
dysaphia
peepshow paper stone scissors gam

Maximum circus fruit
(based on Peep/Show search terms – as sug

Anne Gorrick

Acts, posters, costumes
Free Johnny Cash from predetermined c
Dog kites do Brazil
Dolliecrave in doll school
School island, scandalous folders
Field studies in a deaf font for lady macl
For you I will party
Your legs in consideration, broadcast th
Vindicator and restless, refuses patdow
Dress tomorrow in photos of yourself
Plus-sized pink suits slay dragons
Foot locker, meat dress, bad romance, r
Peeptoe, preparing newly woven silk, pe
Sunflower cake diorama
Show some mercy in your shooting game
Show a machine gun cartridge with a bel
Show a machine that makes marbles
Show Tokyo on a map
Show science projects with

When I went back later to edit the entire manuscript, I found that a phrase from this same poem became the beginning of another poem, and ended up being the start of another entire manuscript of poems...

the porch buried me between failures and bread
qual shades of Johnsian greys
in and France, between spoiled meat and bleach
e song sung in zebra cocktail rings
tion in Massapequa
es, volcanos, radios
rs, mad spellers of the world untie
ells that work, spells to become a vampire
rses for beginners
someone fall in love with you or become a mermaid
veight or get what you want
swallowing, and trouble sleeping
riend in free pools
now affection?
wallowed by hippo
vers transferred to canvas
by money, artists that allow trust
ged the world

beginning of next book!

Did you envision this collection as a collection or understand your process as writing specifically around a theme while the poems themselves were being written? How or how not?

As you can see, I generally start playing with a processual idea. These processes often generate a book-length text. If the process doesn't seem juicy enough, I'll abandon it before a book happens. In this case, I kept going and by the end, I became fluent in playing/maneuvering within this generative system. The great thing about this fluency is that after this body of work, I was able to transport it in small amounts, into new work with other generative processes.

What formal structures or other constructive practices (if any) do you use in the creation of your work? Have certain teachers or instructive environments, or readings/writings of other creative people (poets or others) informed the way you work/write?

When I was young, I studied classical piano for nine years, and you start to see how much you can tweak to define sound within a really small confine. I also played a lot of competitive tennis up until a few years ago. You see how many thousands of balls you have to hit before that one perfect shot that you never even knew was possible. I love the Arnold Palmer quote about "the more I practice, the luckier I get." I'm a dabbler in a Chinese body practice (an "internal martial art"), and I love to hike, to feel my body move through landscape, be part of it. I've learned a lot from the poet Robert Kelly about how to construct a life out of writing, art, and music. The Women's Studio Workshop in Rosendale, NY was arms-open-wide to me when I wanted to study visual art to extend my textual work.

I've learned a tremendous amount by collaborating with other writers and artists, as it always extends my textual and visual vocabularies, my fluencies. Lately, my friend Lee Gould has encouraged me to attempt translation, and poet Eduardo Padilla has been my generous and hilarious collaborator. I've been in awe of and very moved by John Bloomberg-Rissman's projects. My collaborations with him have taught me how to integrate various generative processes, so they're not so silo-ed. This was a big leap for me. Working alongside artists Cynthia Winika and Scott Helmes on different projects gave me insights into their fluencies. I also co-curated an electronic journal Peep/Show with poet Lynn Behrendt, and this book owes a debt to the colab. Translator and photographer Charlotte Mandell and I recently published an alternating conversation of photographs and poems. I love to work with other people because I learn so much.

Most recently, I started a deeper investigation into encaustic monotype with artist Paula Roland. This has led down some breathtaking supermagic rabbit holes.

Speaking of monikers, what does your title represent? How was it generated? Talk about the way you titled the book, and how your process of naming (poems, sections, etc) influences you and/or colors your work specifically.

"An Absence so Great and Spontaneous it is Evidence of Light" was a phrase that came out of this generative work. It made me laugh and think both that it would make a great definition of both my mother or the Internet. Most titles come from a line in each poem, and are often deliberately, specifically flat sounding. The flatness belies the antic nature of the work. Like olive green next to magenta.

What does this particular collection of poems represent to you ...as indicative of your method/creative practice? your history? your mission/intentions/hopes/plans?

My work isn't necessarily published in book form in the order it was written. It just happens that way sometimes. So the generative processes in this book that take center stage, have been used in smaller quantities in other books. The processual echolocation in this work was a break from the lyric, but it's interesting how the "I" continues to occur. I've said many times that I wait around for what language comes to tell me. I'm not that interested in controlling the work, or setting out to "say." I'm taking notes.

An outcome of my work at Century House (more about this later in this interview) is that I've become very interested in how failed industry (examples of late stage rapacious capitalism) is eventually colonized by the arts.

This boom and bust cycle has been born out and impacted my family history many times. That the poems in this book are essentially made out of internet detritus bumps into these notions, the alchemical transformation dross into...

What does this book DO (as much as what it says or contains)?

An Absence moves language in a new way, and might make you laugh. Introduces a multi-valent capacity. It might also send a great Fuck You to late stage capitalism, which clearly isn't working for so many people.

What would be the best possible outcome for this book? What might it do in the world, and how will its presence as an object facilitate your creative role in your community and beyond? What are your hopes for this book, and for your practice?

The best possible outcome is that it is read, explored, investigated. It presents an antic, Dadaist joy for the reader.

Let's talk a little bit about the role of poetics and creative community in social activism, in particular in what I call "Civil Rights 2.0," which has remained immediately present all around us in the time leading up to this series' publication. I'd be curious to hear some thoughts on the challenges we face in speaking and publishing across lines of race, age, privilege, social/cultural background, and sexuality within the community, vs. the dangers of remaining and producing in isolated "silos."

There are two parts of my life that I see as practically activist, that help create poem-shaped spaces in the world. First, I've been involved in Century House Historical Society in Rosendale, NY since 2005, and was President from 2009 until 2017. An all-volunteer organization, our mission is to preserve the history of our local cement industry, and we have a little museum, as well as the Widow Jane Mine on our property. But since I became President, I wanted to use the arts more to interrogate the industrial history we preserve. We've had site-sensitive sculpture exhibitions, innovation sound-art programs, and world music concerts including taiko drumming. This year we will host the 28th Annual Subterranean Poetry Festival. Any opportunity we have to create, insert events like this into the horrors of late stage capitalism, makes space for resistance, comfort and joy.

Secondly, my day job is that I work in Financial Aid at a community college. I feel strongly about debt being a form of slavery, and that financial literacy is the best way to avoid students constraining their creative lives with unreasonable educational debt. I often work with baby writers and artists, and many marginalized students to help them come to school, in the hopes they become part of our larger creative community. I want our student's voices to be heard. Education is resistance.

In the end, the poem is a radical, investigative act. It's a field where we can explore and interrogate every fluidity, chance, accident, cloud formation, every precariousness. Anything that is slippery. Anything at all. It's a purely free space. Which is the start of something essential, non-hierarchical. Deleuze's "yes and." As Robert Kelly wrote, "Scorn nothing. Write everything." Praise and witness.

ALSO BY ANNE GORRICK

My Beauty is an Occupiable Space
a collaboration with John Bloomberg-Rissman

The Olfactions: Poems on Perfume

In|Filtration: An Anthology of Innovative Poetry from the Hudson River Valley
co-edited with Sam Truitt

A's Visuality

I-Formation (Book Two)

I-Formation (Book One)

Kyotologic: the Pillow Book Poems

"Swans, the ice," she said
a collaboration with Cynthia Winika

The Operating System uses the language "print document" to differentiate from the book-object as part of our mission to distinguish the act of documentation-in-book-FORM from the act of publishing as a backwards-facing replication of the book's agentive *role* as it may have appeared the last several centuries of its history. Ultimately, I approach the book as TECHNOLOGY: one of a variety of printed documents (in this case, bound) that humans have invented and in turn used to archive and disseminate ideas, beliefs, stories, and other evidence of production.

Ownership and use of printing presses and access to (or restriction of printed materials) has long been a site of struggle, related in many ways to revolutionary activity and the fight for civil rights and free speech all over the world. While (in many countries) the contemporary quotidian landscape has indeed drastically shifted in its access to platforms for sharing information and in the widespread ability to "publish" digitally, even with extremely limited resources, the importance of publication on physical media has not diminished. In fact, this may be the most critical time in recent history for activist groups, artists, and others to insist upon learning, establishing, and encouraging personal and community documentation practices. Hear me out.

With The OS's print endeavors I wanted to open up a conversation about this: the ultimately radical, transgressive act of creating PRINT / DOCUMENTATION in the digital age. It's a question of the archive, and of history: who gets to tell the story, and what evidence of our life, our behaviors, our experiences are we leaving behind? We can know little to nothing about the future into which we're leaving an unprecedentedly digital document trail — but we can be assured that publications, government agencies, museums, schools, and other institutional powers that be will continue to leave BOTH a digital and print version of their production for the official record. Will we?

As a (rogue) anthropologist and long time academic, I can easily pull up many accounts about how lives, behaviors, experiences — how THE STORY of a time or place — was pieced together using the deep study of correspondence, notebooks, and other physical documents which are no longer the norm in many lives and practices. As we move our creative behaviors towards digital note taking, and even audio and video, what can we predict about future technology that is in any way assuring that our stories will be accurately told – or told at all? How will we leave these things for the record?

In these documents we say:
WE WERE HERE, WE EXISTED, WE HAVE A DIFFERENT STORY

- Lynne DeSilva-Johnson, Founder/Creative Director
THE OPERATING SYSTEM, Brooklyn NY 2018

RECENT & FORTHCOMING
OS PRINT / DOCUMENTS 2018-19

Ark Hive-Marthe Reed [2019]
A Bony Framework for the Tangible Universe-D. Allen [kin(d)*, 2019]
Śnienie / Dreaming - Marta Zelwan/Krystyna Sakowicz,
(Polish-English/dual-language) trans. Victoria Miluch [glossarium, 2019]
Opera on TV-James Brunton [kin(d)*, 2019]
Alparegho: Pareil-À-Rien / Alparegho, Like Nothing Else - Hélène Sanguinetti
(French-English/dual-language), trans. Ann Cefola [glossarium, 2019]
Hall of Waters-Berry Grass [kin(d)*, 2019]
High Tide Of The Eyes - Bijan Elahi (Farsi-English/dual-language)
trans. Rebecca Ruth Gould and Kayvan Tahmasebian [glossarium, 2019]
I Made for You a New Machine and All it Does is Hope - Richard Lucyshyn [2019]
Illusory Borders-Heidi Reszies [2019]
Transitional Object-Adrian Silbernagel [kin(d)*, 2019]
A Year of Misreading the Wildcats [2019]

An Absence So Great and Spontaneous It Is Evidence of Light - Anne Gorrick [2018]
The Book of Everyday Instruction - Chloe Bass [2018]
Executive Orders Vol. II - a collaboration with the Organism for Poetic Research [2018]
One More Revolution - Andrea Mazzariello [2018]
The Suitcase Tree - Filip Marinovich [2018]
Chlorosis - Michael Flatt and Derrick Mund [2018]
Sussuros a Mi Padre - Erick Sáenz [2018]
Sharing Plastic - Blake Nemec [2018]
The Book of Sounds - Mehdi Navid (Farsi dual language, trans. Tina Rahimi) [glossarium, 2018]
In Corpore Sano : Creative Practice and the Challenged Body [Anthology, 2018]
Abandoners - Lesley Ann Wheeler [2018]
Jazzercise is a Language - Gabriel Ojeda-Sague [2018]
Return Trip / Viaje Al Regreso - Israel Dominguez;
(Spanish-English dual language) trans. Margaret Randall [glossarium, 2018]
Born Again - Ivy Johnson [2018]
Attendance - Rocío Carlos and Rachel McLeod Kaminer [2018]
Singing for Nothing - Wally Swist [2018]
The Ways of the Monster - Jay Besemer [2018]
Walking Away From Explosions in Slow Motion - Gregory Crosby [2018]
Field Guide to Autobiography - Melissa Eleftherion [2018]
Kawsay: The Flame of the Jungle - María Vázquez Valdez
(Spanish-English dual language) trans. Margaret Randall [glossarium, 2018]

2018 CHAPBOOK SERIES:

Want-catcher - Adra Raine; We, The Monstrous - Mark DuCharme;
Greater Grave - Jacq Greyja; Needles of Itching Feathers - Jared Schickling

DOC U MENT

/däkyəmənt/

First meant "instruction" or "evidence," whether written or not.

noun - a piece of written, printed, or electronic matter that provides information or evidence or that serves as an official record
verb - record (something) in written, photographic, or other form
synonyms - paper - deed - record - writing - act - instrument

[*Middle English, precept, from Old French, from Latin documentum, example, proof, from docre, to teach; see dek- in Indo-European roots.*]

Who is responsible for the manufacture of value?

Based on what supercilious ontology have we landed in a space where we vie against other creative people in vain pursuit
of the fleeting credibilities of the scarcity economy, rather than
freely collaborating and sharing openly with each other
in ecstatic celebration of MAKING?

While we understand and acknowledge the economic pressures and fear-mongering that threatens to dominate and crush the creative impulse, we also believe that ***now more than ever we have the tools to relinquish agency via cooperative means,*** fueled by the fires of the Open Source Movement.

Looking out across the invisible vistas of that rhizomatic parallel country we can begin to see our community beyond constraints,
in the place where intention meets
resilient, proactive, collaborative organization.

Here is a document born of that belief, sown purely of imagination and will. When we document we assert. We print to make real, to reify our being there. When we do so with mindful intention to address our process, to open our work to others, to create beauty in words in space, to respect and acknowledge the strength of the page we now hold physical, a thing in our hand,
we remind ourselves that, like Dorothy:
we had the power all along, my dears.

THE PRINT! DOCUMENT SERIES

is a project of
the trouble with bartleby
in collaboration with
the operating system

CPSIA information can be obtained
at www.ICGtesting.com
Printed in the USA
BVHW011406080319
541787BV00011B/2/P